The Perc Foundation
Yesterday & Today

A Memoir
by Olive Surtees

> All profits from the sale of this book will be directed to the charitable funds of The Percy Hedley Foundation.

Previous page: The original key preserved by the Foundation which was used by Mrs Frank Wilkin to open the front door of Hampeth Lodge for the first time following purchase in 1953 by the Parents Association of the Friends of Spastic Children, North East Area.

Front cover: John Harrison.

Back cover: Stuart Dawson.

Contents

Foreword

In 2008 the Secretary of State for Schools, Children and Families launched a new initiative for children with disability which was entitled "Aiming High". A similar strategy emerged from the Department of Health and between them almost £500m of new taxpayers' money was made available for this previously very disadvantaged group of children and their families.

It is difficult writing this in 2011 when society has the view that the Welfare State should take care of everything to understand what it was like 60 years ago. The war had just ended, the NHS had just started and there were huge gaps in our medical knowledge compared to now. But a need for education of children with cerebral palsy was recognised and instead of waiting for the state to help, a partnership of health care professionals, teachers and most importantly parents set about providing the vital resources that children needed. There was no ready-made model on which to base their proposed service but they were fortunate enough to have visionary medical and other health care professionals who began to develop about what we would now call a "centre of excellence". Olive Surtees is to be congratulated on putting together such a magnificent account of this pioneering institution. When she was discussing the project with Dr Errington Ellis, the school's first medical director, he asked her who would want to read it? The answer is not only those who have been involved over almost sixty years but a wider audience of anyone who cares about the community in which they live. Anyone reading this should be inspired to look at what they can do to provide help and support for those who need it most.

It is a tale of a big ambition which has been more than adequately fulfilled. From humble beginnings the Percy Hedley Foundation has built up a service which is the envy of many other areas. They recognised at an early stage the importance of children growing up and that service and support could not stop at school leaving age. Adult Education and employment have led the way once again as an inspiration to many other areas where these issues are sadly neglected. There are many heart warming stories of individual children and members of staff. I was pleased to see mention of many of the services which are so vital to the care of children with spasticity but who so often remain as "back room boys".

Colin Peacock of Peacocks Medical Group has been a huge support to Percy Hedley not only providing vital orthotic equipment to enable young people to make the best of their disabilities but also providing employment for the occasional graduate of the school. The school was opened in the centre of a residential area in east Newcastle and the local community has always welcomed them. It is good to see mention of the 8th Benton cub scouts who were based at Percy Hedley but who have taken a full part in scouting activities in Northumbria.

Sir Alan Craft

How many schools can boast of three Olympic gold medals? This small book is a wonderful tribute to the many hundreds of people in the north of England who have attended the school, worked in it or financially supported it over so many years.

The north of England has a long track record of identifying important medical and social issues and then doing something about them. My predecessor as Professor of Child Health at Newcastle University was one of the many inspirations behind the founding of Percy Hedley. In talking of his own Department he wrote that companionship and not achievement must be the driving force behind any success. It is clear from Olive's account that both have been achieved magnificently at Percy Hedley.

Sir Alan Craft
The James Spence Professor of Child Health
at the University of Newcastle upon Tyne

Acknowledgements

I am very grateful to Jim Ferris, Chief Executive 1995-2008, and his wife Sarah for their encouragement, criticism and advice on the preparation of this manuscript. I am indebted to the late Dr Errington Ellis for giving time and attention to my search for historical information as well as bequeathing slides, documents and booklets. Without support and cooperation from Mr Des Bustard, fundraiser I would not have had access to archival material held by The Percy Hedley Foundation. I wish also to thank Dr Matt Ridley for giving permission for extracts of "The Babies Hospital" written by Ursula Viscountess Ridley to be included.

Without the cooperation of many staff and pupils it would not have been possible to produce this book. I am particularly grateful to the family of Stephen Lawrence Darke who have given permission to publish their early correspondence. Also I thank Mr Colin Peacock for supplying the early history of his Company. I count myself most fortunate that I was able to meet Mrs Hilda Shield, First Deputy Head Teacher, whose retention of valuable information remained constant until her death in January 2011.

Throughout the preparation of this history I have had the good fortune of working with Angela Elliott, Secretary to the Chief Executive who has patiently typed and rearranged the script. Also I thank Ed Turner, Media Development Officer for his contribution by selecting and improving the quality of photographs. My appreciation goes to my publisher Andrew Clark of Summerhill Books for his valuable contribution by completing the work. And to Kath Smith of the Remembering the Past, Resourcing the Future Project at North Shields Library for her initial advice and encouragement.

It was never my intention to publish a detailed historical chronicle. This book should be regarded as a personal account only. Within this context I have attempted to encapsulate personalities, who in various ways caught the spirit of the place at the time. To Sir Alan Craft who provided the foreword, to members of the Percy Hedley staff past and present, old pupils who sent in personal memories without whose accounts and assistance this book would not have materialised. My sincere thanks to them all.

Olive Surtees

Where copyright has been obvious permission has been sought from those holders.

Introduction

The Percy Hedley Foundation provides specialist services for disabled people in the North East of England. Celebrating fifty years of progress in 2003, Executive Committee Chair Dr R L Townsin, paid tribute to the pioneering initiatives of its founders, and a "truly fascinating story of … 50 years … [of] … outstanding commitment". Dr Townsin highlights the key characteristic of the Foundation's success, which is an undiluted continuity with its founding ethos by successive generations of staff: to promote the rights, needs and aspirations of children and adults with cerebral palsy and communication difficulties. Since 2003, continuing dedication to that ethos has driven the provision of a new Senior School, a Disability Sports Academy, a Post-16 Centre, Employability and Training services and, following a merger with the Northern Counties School For The Deaf, a Total Communication facility and a College.

To understand the root of the Foundation's continuing success, it is important to revisit the context of its inception, and the driving motivations of its founders. The opening of the Percy Hedley School and Clinic on February 16th, 1953, Newcastle upon Tyne, with twelve children with cerebral palsy, was the result of a complex fusion of historical and social circumstances and philanthropic initiative. The inauguration of the Babies' Hospital and the Home for Crippled Children, for example, reflected key parallel developments in the late 19th and early 20th centuries to found regional family services provision in the harsh and turbulent socio-economic environment of the North East.

Until the late forties, early fifties there had been inconsistent attention given to children with cerebral palsy. Moreover, treatment when it was available focused on surgery, splinting, massage and exercises. There was a paucity of knowledge in this area, also a particularly virulent poliomyelitis epidemic required urgent attention at that time. This therefore rendered the needs of children with congenital conditions as secondary. Once a vaccine was introduced and polio cases were reduced there was a surge of interest in new methods to remedy the situation. This did not focus on treatment alone but on the education and management of the child in equal measure. The treatment, management and education of neurologically disordered children was a neglected area.

Three Headteachers, Jim Ferris, David Johnston and Norman Stromsoy celebrating 50 years of achievement.

Year upon year since the opening of the Percy Hedley School and Clinic in 1953 there has been an annual publication – The Percy Hedley Yearbook – which is circulated in the North East; to parents, local authorities, businesses, visitors, past pupils, staff and others. To my knowledge only one complete set of copies published between 1953 – 1993 has survived. This being due to the diligence and foresight of Hilda Shield, the first deputy headteacher at the school who has since bequeathed them to the Foundation.

Within all those pages lies a fascinating tale which I feel is of socio/historical importance – not to be lost. But who reads a yearbook, retains the information therein and then relates it to the next publication a year hence? Who, I wonder, reads and relates the accounts, the activities and achievements of today with those of yesterday? A yearbook may be lost, gather dust or even be discarded and a really true exciting story spanning fifty years goes by untold. But one single continuous account might just survive and that survival would ensure that all who became involved in the Percy Hedley Foundation, now and in the future, could take pride in its humble beginnings, its pioneering spirit, development and achievements if only they knew the whole story. Moreover, that those who participate within or without the organisation, as an employee in any role, as a committee member, a parent or a sponsor would understand better today and tomorrow the part they were playing and that their part had meaning and was truly valued. This history demonstrates the importance of all the parts contributing to the Foundation we see today.

Historical tales are most meaningful when recounted by one or more who were there; those who experienced the pains and pleasures, those who knew the children, their parents and played their part on the same stage. That number is dwindling; I was fortunate enough to be there at that time and now privileged to tell the tale.

In order to proceed I made my initial contact with Dr Ellis, the first Medical Director, to discuss the idea in December 2005. After pondering for a while and questioning who would want to read it he noted my enthusiasm to write it, if for no other reason for it to rest in the archives of the Percy Hedley Foundation. From hereon he gave me every encouragement and the following year we met on three occasions. He prepared meticulous historical notes, donated all his slides and many documents before he died in July 2006. Without his support and co-operation I could not have proceeded. Dr Ellis made very clear that a history of the Percy Hedley Foundation could not be divorced from that of the Babies' Hospital (see appendix) and the W J Sanderson Orthopaedic Hospital School. All are interconnected and form an integral part of the social history of the North East of which the Percy Hedley Foundation can be proud.

Mr. Frank Wilkin, T.D.

Extract from the 1953 year book.

Parent Power

Although cerebral palsy had been identified and categorised, first by William Little in 1893 and re-categorised by Sigmund Freud in 1923, it was not until the 1940s that serious attention was paid to this condition. A successful vaccination programme had resulted in a decline in cases of poliomyelitis and this allowed for more time and attention to be directed towards cerebral palsy.

In 1952 one of the largest charities in Britain emerged: The National Spastics' Society which changed its name to SCOPE in 1994. A small group of parents of children with cerebral palsy living through a difficult post-war period were striving to create a school for them. By 1960 they had made considerable progress; one hundred and twenty local groups had been formed as well as seventy special schools and centres opened which were delivering different services for different categories. In 1964 Richard Dimbleby, an eminent British broadcaster, assisted the National Spastics' Society to produce a book entitled *Every Eight Hours* which gave a history of the society and referred to the frequency a child was born with cerebral palsy in the UK. These combined efforts were generating public interest and awareness of the condition and the associated problems.

Funding was provided for the purchase of some large country houses in various parts of the UK; Ingfield Manor in Sussex, Irton Hall in Cumbria, Hawksworth Hall in Yorkshire and Craig-y-parc in Wales. Moreover, other charities were emerging with similar aims and objectives. It is not surprising, therefore, that there was lively activity by a similar group in the North East. Like so many ventures calling for attention to a neglected group of children it is parents who most often spearhead the cause. In the W J Sanderson Orthopaedic Hospital School, Gosforth there was a minority group of cerebral palsy children whose parents had discussed with Mr Herbert Severs, the Headteacher, whether there was any possibility of separation for this minority group so that their particular educational and medical needs could be met more adequately. Mr and Mrs Stephen Darke, whose eldest son Stephen Lawrence had been born with cerebral palsy, were very active members of this group.

Three years after their wedding at St Theresa's Church, Heaton Road, Newcastle, Molly Darke had received a letter from the War Office notifying her that her husband Stephen had been killed so he was never going to see his first born son, Stephen Lawrence. Following a month of mourning Molly received a second letter: no explanation was given for the initial error but Stephen Darke was in fact alive but was by now a prisoner of war in Italy. For the next four years he spent time in different prisoner of war camps in Italy and Germany before returning home to the news, hidden from him for five years, that his son Stephen had been diagnosed with cerebral palsy. Molly had withheld this information not wishing to cause him more anxiety than he had endured already.

Private Stephen Darke 149th Field Ambulance RAME and his wife Molly on their wedding day.

In their search for an educational placement for their son they had encountered many obstacles (see correspondence pages 128-130). Undeterred and undaunted they decided to insert an advertisement in the Evening Chronicle – inviting parents of cerebral palsy children in a similar plight to themselves to make themselves known, to come forward and give impetus to the cause.

This resulted in a very historical meeting held at the YMCA, Blackett Street on 2nd December 1949 which was convened and chaired by the Lord Mayor of Newcastle, Alderman H Charlton JP "to consider the establishment of a unit for the treatment and education of

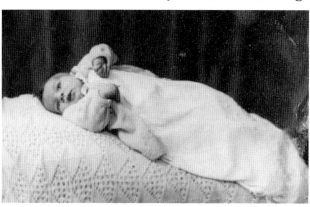

Stephen Lawrence Darke born January 8th 1942.

cerebral palsy children". Those present included Dr Donald Brown, Mr Herbert Severs, Mr S Phillips representing the Director of Education, Dr J B Tilley, Dr W S Walton, Dr Muriel Morley, Mr Frank Wilkin and Mr G B Lauder. Mr Lauder put forward the case for establishing a school and referred to the volume of press publicity that he had received in the past few months. He spoke of this facility benefiting the whole of the North East.

There were some present who resisted radical change and being cautious suggested only a small unit at first. Also, that teaching and medical staff required should be the responsibility of the Local Education Authority and the Local Health Authority. Moreover, that as a first step a prefabricated building could be erected in the grounds of the W J Sanderson Hospital, Gosforth. This proposal was rejected and the Parents' Association pushed harder for a separate school. By 1949 they were on the way to achieving their goal.

SPASTICS SCHOOL NEARS READINESS

Expected to be open early in New Year

By HAROLD WILLIAMSON, Our Education Correspondent

RAPID progress is being made at the Percy Hedley School for Spastic Children, Newcastle, which is expected to open early in the New Year, appoint the teaching staff and make plans to keep the school in the public eye.

The school has come into being as a result of voluntary efforts on the part of the Friends of the Spastic Children, North-Eastern Area, and their work must continue if the school is to be kept going.

Viscountess Ridley and Professor Sir James Spence, Nuffield Professor of Child Health, Durham University, are to make an appeal in the B.B.C. programme, "The Week's Good Cause," on Sunday, February 1.

"A WONDERFUL FOUNDATION"

The Duchess of Northumberland, who views the school as "a wonderful foundation," has become patroness and will officiate at the opening ceremony. The date has not yet been fixed.

Newcastle Journal, December 12th 1952.

This was the catalyst for the founding of the Parents' Association of the Friends of the Spastic Children, North East Area. Mr George Lauder was the first Honorary Secretary and once established Mr Frank Wilkin became the first Chairman of the Percy Hedley School.

During this period of intense activity, Stephen and Molly Darke were living in Tenbury Crescent, Benton. It became known locally that the owner of Hampeth Lodge, situated on Station Road, Forest Hall was considering putting his house on the market. Hampeth Lodge was a short walk from Tenbury Crescent so Molly approached the vendor and put forward a good case for a purchase by the Friends of Spastic Children (North East). The vendor resumed the contact after considering the offer, and eventually the purchase was completed. Apart from the house, the location was ideal being in the middle of a local community, adjacent to shops, churches, on a main road and in walking distance of the Railway Station. How the local residents viewed the prospect of a special school in their midst in 1949 one can only speculate. In spite of all the publicity attached to this venture ignorance about the nature of cerebral palsy abounded.

The Parents' Association brought together an influential Medical Advisory Committee with Professor Sir James Spence of the University Department of Child Health as its Chairman. Dr Errington Ellis was First Assistant in the Department at that time and in December 1952 Sir James Spence told him that the Parents' Association had given him a list of three

Hampeth Lodge, Forest Hall.

hundred children with cerebral palsy and that he wanted each child examined by a paediatrician, an orthopaedic surgeon and a psychologist and he asked him to organise this. Dr Ellis asked how long he had got and he replied, "three weeks". Sir James and Dr Ellis saw the first five children together, and then Dr Ellis went on to see the remaining children on his own, which formed the basis of his MD thesis. The requirements before a child could be admitted to the School were, firstly, that the child should have cerebral palsy which gave him so great a physical disability that he could not be cared for in any other school in the area and, secondly, that he should have sufficient intelligence to benefit from normal education. Dr Errington Ellis was appointed as Medical Director of the school and held this post until 1986. He was succeeded by Dr Mary Gibson, a Paediatric Neurologist, who retired in 2009.

Dr Ellis chairing a staff meeting.

Dr Muriel Morley was instrumental in establishing speech therapy as a recognised profession and she became Chairman of the School Governors.

On 16th February 1953, twelve children were admitted to the School. Because it was anticipated that the children would be unsettled, particularly at night, Muriel Morley arranged a rota of speech therapists to sit up at night to comfort them.

The Management Committee of the School agreed that it should serve the area of the Newcastle Regional Hospital Board, and from surveys which were made subsequently in the region, it was estimated that about one-tenth of all children with cerebral palsy should be admitted to a special school designed for them. Extensions to the School were planned so that it could accommodate twenty day children of school age living on Tyneside, forty resident children of school age from homes scattered throughout the rest of the Northern Region, and twelve young children in a nursery group. With a total of seventy two places it was believed that the Percy Hedley School would be able to cater for all those children between the ages of two and sixteen years living in the Northern Region who needed to be admitted. These extensions to the School were completed in 1959.

Soon after the School opened in 1953 Dr Rennie, the Medical Officer of Health for Carlisle, asked Dr Ellis to assess the needs of a number of children with cerebral palsy living in Carlisle. He agreed to go to the George Street Clinic each Tuesday afternoon to see two children with their parents between 2.00 and 4.00 pm. Dr Ellis then asked him to invite to tea all the professionals involved with each child – school teacher, physiotherapist, speech therapist, educational psychologist – so that discussion could take place about the needs of each child. If it seemed appropriate the child could be admitted with his mother to the clinic at Forest Hall. The next year Dr Fraser, the Medical Officer for Cumberland, asked the Centre to establish similar clinics in Whitehaven and Workington and at a later date clinics were held at Dryburn, Durham, Middlesbrough and Sunderland. Val Cullotty, Superintendent Physiotherapist at the Percy Hedley School, usually accompanied Dr Ellis to these clinics. At a later date Doris Peaps, social worker at the Percy Hedley Clinic, went as well so that good contacts were developed with those treating and caring for cerebral palsied children throughout the region.

Because it was realised that a lot of attention was being paid to children of 'normal' intelligence the team requested a visit to Prudhoe and later Northgate Hospitals where the staff were trying to modify the handling and treatment of many severely disabled children living there.

From the beginning the team had the support of a strong medical advisory committee, all of whom agreed to see children with their parents at the Percy Hedley Centre:-

Mr Michael James (Consultant Orthopaedic Surgeon at the Sanderson Hospital) who agreed to advise on splints and braces. Because he was dissatisfied with the results of orthopaedic surgery in cerebral palsied children he agreed not to operate on any of the children referred to our clinic for a trial period of five years.

Professor Sir John Walton (Professor of Neurology at Newcastle University)

Mr Stanley Arkle (Consultant Ophthalmologist in charge of the Department of Ophthalmology at the RVI)

Dr Israel Kolvin (Consultant Child Psychiatrist, Fleming Memorial Hospital)

The first task was to select children from Sir James Spence's list of three hundred for admission to the School. Dr Ellis saw all the children and their parents himself, usually with Val Culloty, physiotherapist, Enid Taylor, speech therapist, and Molly Cooknell, nursery school teacher. The decisions were therefore 'multi-disciplinary'. Later they were able to expand this method of working by admitting children and their mothers into play groups, which allowed more detailed assessment.

Children were referred to them from Local Education Authorities and it seemed sensible to limit activities to the area of the Newcastle Regional Hospital Board, which included the counties of Northumberland, Durham, part of the North Riding of Yorkshire, Cumberland and North Westmorland, with a total population of 3,000,000 (1,000,000 living on Tyneside, 1,000,000 living on Teesside and 1,000,000 living in homes scattered throughout the rest of the region. The aim was to establish a Register of all children with cerebral palsy living in the region. This aim was never achieved but it was felt that the surveys in Northumberland, Tyneside and Carlisle were sufficiently complete to allow for extrapolation of

The Clinic where 50 children received outpatient treatment.

16

The School Wing where 16 Residents and 20 Day Pupils were taught.

findings to the rest of the region, and so to plan the extension of the School to meet the needs of the region.

To accommodate the expanding clinic services, the Percy Hedley Centre received in 1953 all the money raised by the Newcastle University students during their annual Rag Week. This enabled the Centre to add to the School a wing with additional rooms on the ground floor for therapists and three bedrooms and a sitting room on the first floor. It allowed for the admission of children with their mothers for a few days at a time. If younger or older children could not be left at home their mother could bring them with her to stay in the clinic. At times fathers or grandmothers were also admitted. If they lived near enough to the clinic the parents could return with their children at weekly, fortnightly or monthly intervals. If they lived at a distance they could return to stay in the clinic for a few days every three or four months. The Regional Hospital Board accepted that if these children were not seen in the Percy Hedley Clinic they would be seen in hospital clinics elsewhere in the region. They made a grant towards the running costs of the Percy Hedley Clinic where about one hundred children were treated regularly in the course of a year.

In 1971 with the support of Professor Donald Court, Professor of Child Health at the University of Newcastle, the work of the Percy Hedley Clinic was moved to a purpose built unit in Professor Court's department where its facilities could be available to children with a wider range of handicaps, and where the students of the many disciplines involved could observe and be taught.

A Chance Encounter

Stephen Lawrence Darke and I have known each other for sixty years. We met first of all in the W J Sanderson Hospital in 1951 when I was training as a physiotherapist at the Royal Victoria Infirmary, Newcastle. It was during a one month placement that I was detailed to go to a small seven year old boy with very bright eyes, lying coiled up in a cot bed who was underdeveloped for his age. He had a good head of very dark hair; he was attractive but unable to speak and I had been instructed to give him passive movements. That was all I had ever seen any therapist do for cerebral palsied children in the early fifties. Stephen and I struck up a good relationship and spent a fair amount of time playing. I never met his parents at that time and eight more years passed before I met Stephen Lawrence again.

I met Neil Murray for the first time during my training in the Physiotherapy Department in the RVI. Neil was seventeen at the time and was attending for his weekly treatment session. As well as having a severe motor (movement) problem affecting arms and legs he had a speech problem too so communication proved difficult. Nevertheless we did get by and struck up a good relationship. He sparkled and had much to tell. So what did the therapist do for Neil? Suspended him on a "Guthrie Smith Suspension Apparatus". This was a large metal frame positioned above a couch from which you could hook springs at any point. Canvas cuffs were placed around each limb and the trunk. The springs were attached to the cuffs just like a curtain tie-back. Neil had his whole body suspended about six centimetres above the couch by the time he was hooked up. The aim was to create a state of relaxation, so there he remained for the next half hour. He did not complain. Surgery and splinting were also used in the fifties for selected cases but not with the refinement and selection available today.

Following qualification, I was appointed as a basic grade physiotherapist at the W J Sanderson Hospital School. Stephen Lawrence had moved on by then but I did meet a four year old, Tommy Leighton. Tommy had to struggle with great difficulty using full length crutches and he was not a happy boy.

Stephen, Neil and Tommy are residents today in Chipchase House, the residential accommodation provided by the Percy Hedley Foundation for adults.

During that year, 1953, I did hear talk of "this new place, Percy Hedley School". Mixed views abounded about the prospects for success or its ultimate survival. No-one knew the newly appointed Irish Superintendent Physiotherapist, Val Culloty. It was not expected that anymore could be done for children with cerebral palsy beyond what was being done already. On reflection I do not think I took much notice. This new school and the exodus of a small core of W J Sanderson staff did not have much relevance to the future life and career path I had in mind. I moved on and, between 1954 and 1959 after working in general hospitals outside the area, I returned to the North East and was accepted for a junior part-time post at the Percy Hedley School.

The next few years were daunting, involving a fair amount of new learning; expanding neurological knowledge, grasping unfamiliar treatment techniques and taking account of social circumstances as well as assessing the learning ability of each child on one's list. Added to this was learning how to relate to parents and build up good lines of communication. Working in a school was unfamiliar territory and multi-disciplinary co-operation was essential, requiring a high level of diplomacy. These are skills learnt only through experience over time and the opportunities were boundless.

Two months before I was appointed Dorothy Thorpe had joined the Physiotherapy Department and was in a similar position to myself. She was twelve years older, married with two sons and had not been employed for a few years. Dorothy was the second daughter of missionaries living and working in Sri Lanka where she was educated until she was twelve years old. As well as physiotherapy training she held an Orthopaedic Nursing certificate. As a result she was given additional remuneration and responsibility for orthopaedic appliances and management of the weekly orthotic clinic when Mr Bill Craddock visited from the firm of J C Peacock and Son. We learnt together and remained close friends until her death in 2003.

Dorothy Thorpe treating a child with hemiplegia.

Percy Hedley and the School

Percy Hedley died in 1941. He was never personally involved in any way with a project which would bear his name. He was born at Chirton, North Shields on 20th January 1865 the only son of John and Mary Hedley. His father was a draper. Percy Hedley trained as a marine engineer and married Lillian Dove, the daughter of John Dove, the builders' merchant. They did not have any children.

Mr Percy Hedley.

Percy and Lillian Hedley emigrated to South Africa and there they prospered but on the death of his wife, Percy Hedley returned to England, initially to London and finally in 1936 to his native North East. He took a lease on an estate house in Carham, close to the church where he was a regular worshipper and where he is buried.

Percy Hedley had decided to create a Trust – The Percy Hedley Will Trust – and leave all his money to be used for charitable purposes in the North East. Those who benefitted were Abbeyfield, Anchor Housing and the Percy Hedley Foundation.

The story goes that it was a chance encounter in the Blackbird Pub, Ponteland that resulted in the Parents' Association benefitting from this particular Trust. Mr Frank Wilkin and others came to be in conversation with the solicitor responsible for selection and distribution.

With the accumulation of funds and the Percy Hedley Trust, the Parents' Association were able to negotiate the terms and purchase of Hampeth Lodge, Station Road, Forest Hall, Newcastle. This was a modest Victorian house set in its own grounds which was re-named, appropriately, the Percy Hedley School, after a man who never knew how his accumulated wealth would benefit so many or that his name would become so well known in the region.

Four experienced teachers working in the W J Sanderson Orthopaedic Hospital School were well placed at the right time to ignite the education process in the Percy Hedley School.

Mr Harry Severs, the Headteacher, had been closely involved with parents and the negotiations between education and medical authorities. Aged sixty-two he was nearing retirement but the following twelve years proved to be a very active and exciting period of his life.

Mrs Molly Cauldwell was already responsible for a class of children with cerebral palsy so she was an obvious choice to be appointed as the first Headteacher.

Mr Harry Severs.

Molly Cooknell was an infants' school teacher and all three were most enthusiastic about embarking on a new challenge. The fourth teacher invited to join them, Mrs Hilda Shield, had some reservations as she was more involved with children with specific physical handicaps. It was only when she learnt that adults might be admitted to the W J Sanderson Centre that she threw her weight behind the cause and was appointed Deputy Headteacher. Hilda was a war widow with a young daughter living in Denton Burn on the west side of the city which involved a long journey daily to reach Forest Hall.

This quartet had particular educational and psychological advantages for this challenge and future stability of the school. Other appointments could not fail to fall in with their management style. They were a ready made team in an ideal location on Station Road, Forest Hall. They were in the centre of a busy community, near a main road with bus and train services giving easy access to the city and the coast.

Initially the three senior teachers spent time with Dr Ellis at the Royal Victoria Infirmary observing new referrals and the assessment procedure. They had to learn much more about

Molly Cauldwell.

cerebral palsy and the numerous associated problems which would affect the ability of the children to learn. They visited different places, and talked to many different people about the project, their ambitions and problems and in so doing engendered support and publicity.

When the school opened twelve children were admitted. It was agreed that the Headteacher would be responsible for senior pupils, Hilda Shield for juniors and Molly Cooknell for infants.

Education

The headteacher, Molly Cauldwell, and her deputy, Hilda Shield, together with Molly Cooknell, the infant teacher, did not formulate a precise curriculum as there was no legislation at the time which demanded it. They had to feel their way, learn on the hoof, utilise their combined knowledge to construct a realistic educational infrastructure which would facilitate children's learning at different levels. Funding was limited so they acquired equipment and other items from wherever they could. Some of their initial contacts supplied scrap paper for drawing or materials for craft work. For them, the availability of aids and sophisticated equipment available today would have been a dream. One bright girl with athetosis could not turn pages so Hilda or another child had to do it for her until, on a visit to the Middlesex Hospital, Hilda spotted an electric page turner costing fourteen pounds. The Management Committee was persuaded to buy it and the child gained some independence. There were some children who could not hold a pencil or isolate a finger to type. They were fitted with a 'unicorn' which consisted of a headband with a central spike to strike the keyboard. Others needed support to sit on wooden chairs and maintain an upright posture. Groin

Early Pupils – Norman Johnson, Ronnie Crozier, Doreen Entwhistle and Janette Dawson in 1957.

straps anchored in the centre of the seat held hips at a right angle. A foot rest was fixed to the base and feet were positioned between short parallel wooden strips with straps over to hold the position. Two small wheels attached to the back legs and a metal handle at the top allowed for the chair to be moved when tipped backwards. Added to these restrictions was the use of shoulder straps in some instances.

Ian Crawford on a wooden chair with groin straps in 1966.

Although the curriculum for each group was not specified in detail the aims were clear. The closest contact with parents was encouraged and they were always encouraged to visit and be involved. Without them success was limited. A small group of mothers were enlisted to work voluntarily in the class rooms which proved to be of mutual benefit.

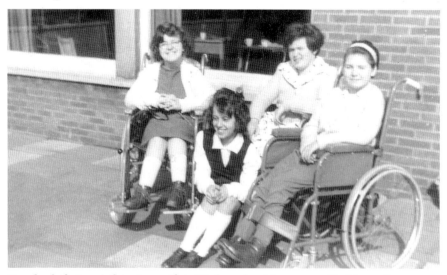

Back, left to right: Jennifer Richards, Maureen Reiling, Joan Bell. Front: Christine Hann in 1966.

There was an on-going regional survey to determine the extent of provision required. The catchment area population totalled 3,000,000 in 1963 so it was estimated that ultimately the maximum intake should not exceed seventy-two pupils which would allow all cerebral palsied children from five Northern counties assessed as 'educable' to be admitted. By 1954 twenty children attended. By 1957 there were twenty-two day pupils and seventeen in residence. In 1959 new

Learning to stand and work with support.

classrooms were ready and seventy-two children were on the register of which ten were under five years in the nursery class. It was now proving possible to increase the numbers and it was accepted that the majority were likely to need education for life.

Rarely did a child transfer into a less specialised school. It was accepted that to be of real value for severely disabled children the curriculum must be broadly based and very practical.

The provision of places in special schools has always been very expensive. By 1959 a school for seventy-two children had been provided at a cost of £100,000 over a six year period and fourteen Local Education Authorities in the region were paying fees to cover the running costs.

In 1953 a strong Medical Advisory Committee, under the chairmanship of Sir James Spence, accepted responsibility for all admissions and discharges from the school. As a result it began its life with a very strong medical bias and without a clear idea of the size of the problems ahead. In 1964 when David Johnston was appointed Headteacher one of his earliest requests was for a full School Inspection to get an accurate assessment of standards of provision.

More specific training courses in Special Education were becoming available. In 1965 one teacher was seconded for one year at the Institute of Education of Newcastle University. Also, to further the knowledge of the learning processes of brain damaged children, the school was co-operating with the Department of Psychological Medicine on a research project. All of which expanded the knowledge base and improved standards of education.

The criteria for admission to the school moved over from medical to educational. As a result the final assessment of educability

Mr David Johnston.

became the defining factor not the extent or severity of the motor disability. The assessment process required care and sound judgement so it was the responsibility of Heads of Departments and the class teacher over a period of one week to record their observations and make recommendations. These included physical and language development, responses in a class room setting to different situations and educational apparatus, all of which were supplemented with results obtained from a battery of psychometric tests (the Vineland Social Maturity Scale, the Minnesota Pre-School Scale, the Merrill-Palmer Scale and for older children the Wechsler Intelligence Scale for Children).

Many more children were attending the clinic adjacent to the school than were attending school full time. The mutual aim was only to admit 10% of the total number of referrals. Many of the out patients joined small groups of 8 – 10 who met once a fortnight for a morning or afternoon under the supervision of Molly Cooknell, the nursery teacher and often assisted by Mrs Ellis, wife of the Medical Director. These groups gave children the opportunity to play, to socialise and communicate. Speech and Physio Therapists too were involved allowing all the facility to observe, assess and ultimately

Alysoun Ellis working with a child.

identify those who would be appropriately placed in school. The groups were discontinued in 1971 when the clinic moved to the Royal Victoria Infirmary and there an official pre-school was established.

By 1967 there were ninety children on the roll ranging in age from three – seventeen years with a wide range of disabilities. There were day children and boarders with a broad range of motor disorders. The learning problems for some children were very severe and although class numbers were small they required specialised remedial attention from the Deputy Headteacher, Hilda Shield. As numbers rose and more remedial work became essential the number of teachers increased.

It was at this time that attention was drawn to a particular group of children described as having minimal brain dysfunction and/or clumsy with severe speech and language disorders. Some presented with reading and emotional difficulties. They were failing in mainstream education and there was little or no provision to address their needs.

Fifteen years of work experience with children with cerebral palsy placed the staff in a favourable position to expand their services and focus attention on fourteen children in school in this particular group. This was the birth of the

Speech and Language Department as well as being a period when additional class rooms became available.

In the early years it was not predicted that many children with cerebral palsy would achieve the attainment levels required for their transfer into mainstream education. However, it became apparent by the late eighties that as a result of early educational and therapeutic intervention more children were in fact able to transfer

Mrs Hilda Shield with Joan Bell and Angela McCluskey in 1960.

before reaching secondary level. As a result the number of children at senior level was reduced but it had the advantage in allowing greater provision for children with speech and language problems.

Mrs Hilda Shield – the first Deputy Head.

Californian teacher, Annie McCulloch (seconded for one year) with her class in 1968.

Two important pieces of legislation surfaced in the eighties which affected education as a whole as well as special education. The 1981 Education Act, which provided a set of procedures for assessing children with special needs, stated the resources needed to meet their needs and where all the criteria could be met. Integration into mainstream education was an aim for as many pupils as possible. This act was not implemented until 1985 and it could be claimed that it has been a bureaucratic minefield for all those involved resulting in controversy and distress for many parents. The 1988 Education Act stated what education should be about in real terms. It also shifted financial responsibility for schools to manage their own budgets with less Local Education Authority involvement.

This act focused the attention of all teachers on the National Curriculum at which point teachers and therapists alike became familiar with 'Statements of Special Educational Needs'. Teachers were required to address the requirements of the National Curriculum and act upon them which was no mean task. It was a very challenging period which resulted in refinement, greater precision regarding curriculum content, recording of outcomes and realistic predictions.

Many who have been associated with the Percy Hedley School, staff, pupils and parents in particular, recount with real pleasure and appreciation the voluntary contributions made by teachers beyond the classroom. These are just a few of so many examples.

Raymond O'Dowd, senior teacher for twenty-seven years, was a man who remained calm under all adversity. He was unstinting in the time he devoted to driving and assisting wherever he could. He was responsible for the Boys' Club which met weekly for a wide variety of social and sporting activities, outings and holidays. Later the Boys' Club amalgamated with the Junior Girls' Club run by Tricia Rose and together attracted fifty-eight members in all and so it was necessary to divide them and meet every fortnight. Apart from the Girls' Club, Tricia Rose constructed, managed and maintained the school library much appreciated by the children and admired by visitors passing through the school. She was famed for her fund-raising events and coffee evenings to pay for particular outings, holidays or other ventures.

Alwyn Moore, senior teacher for twenty-two years, created the Theatre Club which she ran voluntarily as an evening activity. She had boundless enthusiasm for the arts which she shared with the children and ignited a real interest for a group of nineteen senior pupils. She arranged and accompanied them to the theatre to enjoy a whole range of productions: Shakespeare, Alan Bennett, comedies and musicals. On

Susan Frater and Raymond O'Dowd with the captain of HMS Newcastle.

Alwyn Moore at a Christmas Party with, left to right, Graham Thompson, Calum Wiley and Keith Tweddle.

occasions she was accompanied by Pauline Adair, physiotherapist, who had a particular interest in the ballet. In 1991 Pauline introduced a Movement and Dance Group for girls from the speech and language classes. Added to this Alwyn aimed to create in her pupils a sense of social awareness and a focus on the needs of others. She arranged visits to the homes of housebound senior citizens whereby each child 'adopted' one and built up a friendly relationship which was mutually advantageous.

Susan Frater was, for twenty-five years, the teacher responsible for the Reception class and together with two very capable assistants, Margaret Donkin and Doreen Coxon, had the difficult task of settling new children into school. These were children who had been very dependent on their parents and this was their first parting. This small team demonstrated tolerance and great patience, often over many weeks, before a particular child became settled.

Over and above the daily routine Susan Frater became the leader of the Percy Hedley Cubs which had been introduced initially by a speech therapist. When she left, Susan carried on with help from other speech therapists and many others over time. The 8th Benton Cub Scouts had weekly meetings, sports days, swimming galas, weekend camps and the annual district camp involving about one hundred and forty cubs and sixty helpers. The Old Station, Barrasford had been converted into the 1st Longbenton Activity Centre. Keith Simpson and Michael Ash, two local enthusiastic cub leaders, invited the Percy Hedley Cubs for a weekend. This successful event led on to repeat visits. Other ventures followed, staying in other areas of Northumberland and as a result a lasting relationship between local Cub Scouts and the school was sealed. To this day Keith Simpson continues to offer his voluntary services.

The education of the children stretched well beyond the perimeter of the classroom. There was clear recognition that 'all time' is 'learning time' and we were all involved in the process.

Keith Simpson running the youth club.

Susan Frater and the Cub Scouts.

Ann Lowden, Dorothy Hutchinson (teacher), Elizabeth Doughty (care assistant), Jennifer Richards, Christine Hann, Joan Bell in 1966.

Teacher Joyce Langlands with her group waiting for a helicopter landing from HMS Newcastle in 1991.

Physiotherapy

In 1969 Margaret Barass (Head Physiotherapist 1965-79) described the role of the Physiotherapist in this particular setting in the following terms:

"She should have the wisdom of Solomon, the patience of Job, the heart of a lion, the strength of a horse, the cunning of a fox and the sensitivity of a geiger counter. She should be a practitioner, inventor, comforter, confidante and diplomat, PRO, substitute mother, fount of general knowledge, odd job man and athletic coach. She should have some knowledge of splint making, nursery rhymes, human nature, pop music, local slang, arithmetical formulae, esoteric contemporary games, spelling, television and some physiotherapy".

(1969 Yearbook)

Physiotherapy staff in 1989, Back, left to right Pauline Adair, Gillian Miller, Anne Coates, Karol Lalor, Freda Fish. Front, left to right, Alison Carlisle, Olive Surtees, Liz Potts.

Dorothy Thorpe with Brian Scott learning to use a walking aid in 1965.

The Learning Curve

Professional development was encouraged and supported over the years. Initially, funding was made available for therapists to undertake the two month Bobath Course. Dr Karl and Mrs Bertha Bobath had fled from East Germany at the outset of World War II. Mrs Bobath, a physiotherapist, devised a treatment regime for children with cerebral palsy. While Dr Bobath, a neurologist, provided the scientific evidence to support it and together they established their private clinic and training centre in St John's Wood, London. This was the first recognised post-graduate training course for therapists and doctors involved with cerebral palsy and it attracted students world wide. Val Culloty was the first to be appointed as Superintendent Physiotherapist at the school and embarked on this course immediately. As each new therapist was employed they followed this route. The course gave a clear understanding of early normal child development in all areas of motor, speech and function without which one could not identify the abnormal. From thereon the neurology and treatment techniques were introduced. This was an invaluable experience for what was to follow; not just immediately but over the years when new techniques and other courses became available. It was not easy; the written material proved complicated and visual aids were limited. They were not of today's standards.

Provided with this neurological framework learning never ceased and the teaching came in many forms, at different times throughout the working week and over the years. In their wisdom at the outset the Management Committee, Dr Ellis and the Medical Advisory Committee identified and appointed a small clutch of consultants who agreed to visit on a regular basis. On the first Monday morning of each month Mr Michael James, the orthopaedic surgeon based at the W J Sanderson Hospital School held a clinic with all physiotherapists present regardless of whether they were presenting a child on their list or not. Dr Ellis would provide the background information, a physiotherapist would contribute, describe the particular orthopaedic problem which appeared to be obstructing progress and follow this with a demonstration of the techniques or appliances being used in her therapy sessions. Mr James examined the child describing his findings. Once the child left the room we listened to his explanations and recommendations and were free to ask questions. Parents were present and so we observed his skilful presentation of evidence in layman's language.

Faced with very baffling neurological symptoms Dr Ellis called upon Dr John Walton, consultant neurologist, who in later years became the Dean of Medicine at Newcastle University, followed by his elevation to the House of Lords.

In each case the therapist involved described the problems, her observations and treatment programme. Dr Walton was very articulate, fluent and language flowed with ease and speed. So much so that I could not process all the neurological terminology fast enough and resorted to asking Dr Ellis many questions later.

The system worked very well and had particular advantages for staff and children alike. Also, it was economical in time and money. Parents and children did not have to travel to hospital and be greeted by white coats. They remained on familiar territory with those they knew therefore were more relaxed, more able to listen and absorb information and ask questions. Moreover, they and the therapists were able to construct a relationship and lines of communication with one particular consultant and one hospital only for the vast majority of children who attended the school. Following admission, Dr Ellis would write to any consultant who had been involved with a particular child and ask for their permission to transfer to one of the appointed consultants to the school. To this day that system has been perpetuated.

Following the retirement of Mr James and Dr Walton's promotion to a new role we continued the same pattern with Mr Mike Leonard, orthopaedic surgeon, who was based at the Freeman Hospital and Dr Gardner-Medwin, Neurologist at Newcastle General Hospital.

I will be forever grateful to those consultants who contributed so much to the knowledge base of therapists. From time to time they provided opportunities for visits to the operating theatre to witness particular procedures. We were able to build up lines of communication with therapists working in the hospital who would be responsible for the post operative treatment, as a result in certain cases a child could be discharged in the shortest possible time because the recommended treatment could be carried out in school.

In 1967 quite by chance, a rare opportunity came my way. Pat had been a pupil in school. She had a lively mind and great determination but was thwarted by an array of severe unwanted movements which affected her hands and arms more than any other parts of her body. As a result she was twelve years old before she learnt to walk independently and this she did by shuffling backwards against a wall. Without the advantage of using her hands she bent her knees, pressed feet hard into the floor and levered herself up the wall. Once she gained balance she was able to take steps. This was not the Bobath way and it is doubtful whether this great achievement could be attributed to physiotherapy. In sitting she pressed her most abnormally active arm behind her back. She held a pencil between her toes to write and gained the ability to address an envelope and apply a stamp. Her attempts to fix her moving parts resulted in postural problems and various aches and pains as she matured. We made a hessian waistcoat in an attempt to contain and restrain the offending arm in front. Specific medication was tried but without effect.

Pat left school and became a resident in Chipchase House and with the clever use of her feet was able to work in the workshop. Eventually, she pleaded with Dr Ellis to arrange for the arm to be surgically removed. He resisted such a radical procedure and explained in graphic detail how this would interfere with her ability to balance and walk. However, this was a period when stereotaxic surgery was being advocated for some patients with Parkinson's Disease and Athetoid Cerebral Palsy. A consultation was arranged with Mr John Hankinson, Neurosurgeon at Newcastle General Hospital and he considered that Pat would respond favourably to stereotaxic surgery. This involved making a small hole in the skull then

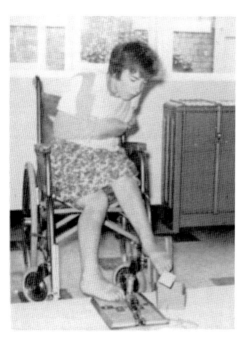

Pat Scott using a guillotine with her feet in 1966.

inserting a fine tube – a cannula – into the lower part of the brain. A freezing solution was injected right onto the damaged area. The initial penetration is painless due to local anaesthesia but the patient has to remain conscious in order to ascertain the immediate effects. This for me proved quite a revelation.

Pat agreed to this surgery but on admission she became so nervous that the plan had to be aborted. After some time and further review she agreed to pursue this course if I was allowed to accompany her to the hospital and remain there until she came out of theatre. This did not present a problem and we arrived one Saturday morning. It did not seem too busy and I had expected to be directed to a waiting room until Pat re-emerged. Not so, Mr Hankinson invited me in to observe if I wished. This was an opportunity not to be missed so quickly I was appropriately dressed. I do not recollect any others present apart from theatre staff, so I was seated next to the surgeon and observing every step being given a sequence of explanations throughout. A series of x-rays hung on the wall and he explained how measurements and calculations were correlated to hit the target area accurately with great precision. This was a lesson in applied geometry for surgical application.

Unfortunately, what appeared to be a good result initially for Pat was short-lived. Over time, Pat came to accept her condition and eventually left Chipchase House when she married and moved out of the area.

The senior staff in the early years made valuable contacts in the UK and abroad. They recognised the importance of interaction, dialogue and exchange visits with other centres. Short courses were attended and major conferences were arranged at the Percy Hedley Centre attended by Dr and Mrs Bobath, Dr Martin Bax, Mr Ronnie McKeith and many other notable professional contributors to the knowledge base in the fifties and sixties. They came from Scope, the Scottish Council, Independent Special Schools and locally; it was a lively pioneering period which served us well over thirty years.

Peacocks

Mr Bill Craddock, the fitter of orthotics from the firm J C Peacocks, attended every week to measure and to fit special footwear and appliances. We learnt much from him about materials, measurements and corrective procedures.

One of the earliest sites of Peacocks was at 22 Collingwood Street, Newcastle where it was managed by John Clint Peacock. He had two sons, Leslie and John Royston, the youngest. Leslie was prepared to take on this fledgling business but died at a very young age. John Royston at this stage had started an optical practice, also in Collingwood Street. When his father died in pretty fast succession to his brother he had to make the decision of abandoning optics and moving into the orthotics and prosthetics business as it was then. He always stated that his optical training brought accuracy of measurement to the business. Collingwood Street was the first site but manufacturing took place in Darn Crook which is the street by St Andrew's Church. The firm moved on and opened up in Claremont Road, opposite the Exhibition Park. This site was superseded by St Thomas' Street in 1968 while the business in Darn Crook and Collingwood Street moved to Friar House around 1962.

Colin Peacock, the present managing director, succeeded his father. Initially he trained as a physiotherapist, this being an appropriate route for the business ahead. In 2000 he moved the business to its current site at Benfield Business Park, the start of a new millennium for Peacocks.

Although there were other competitors in the business of orthotics, surgical and medical equipment, Peacocks have not only survived and served in the North East but expanded to cover the whole of the United Kingdom.

A hundred and eighty people are employed at the Benfield Road site in 2011.

Charlie in 1968 wearing full-length calipers – supplied by Peacocks.

Eddy Weldon, Alan Waite, Joseph Armstrong, Colin Peacock at J.C. Peacocks Benfield Site in 2009.

Bill Craddock was one who joined the company in July 1939 and remained with them until his retirement in 1986. He had come to Peacocks from the W J Sanderson School where he had been a pupil following an attack of polio myelitis. This resulted in permanent paralysis of his lower limbs and the need to wear a full-length caliper and walk with sticks for the rest of his life. It was the training he had in cobbling in his final school years which provided the basic skills for his future career, being responsible for footwear. Bill Craddock was the fitter who served the Percy Hedley Centre until his retirement.

Every Thursday morning he would drive into the car park and Tom Urwin would be on the lookout for him and then go out to assist with carrying his large bag full of appliances into the Physiotherapy Department. Bill was a fine figure of a man. Always positive, strong hands, never downhearted, never daunted by the problems we presented. He was patient, polite and had a wonderful manner with the children.

Two Percy Hedley pupils left school and gained employment with Peacocks and Bill Craddock was very involved with their training during their early years with the company. He proved an excellent teacher as well as being an example and mentor to them. Alan Waite was admitted to school at five years old in 1957 and left in 1969. Joe Armstrong was admitted in 1960 aged four and left school in 1972.

"Alan and Joe are superb employees. They are virtually never off sick and have a great loyalty to the company. Alan has good manual dexterity and initially worked in our leather covering department where he has shown such skill that he now is in charge. Joe had more problems with his hands and we channelled him into administrative work and he is now responsible for inspection within the footwear department. They have a truly magnificent health record which any able-bodied person would be proud of and I regularly talk with pride about their attitude to work. Alan has had sickness problems but he seems to have taken time off as holiday and does everything to be a superb example representative of people with a disability".

Colin Peacock, Managing Director

Apart from life-long service to the company Bill Craddock was very involved with the Newcastle branch of the Polio Fellowship which had premises on Osborne Road, Jesmond. He was an enthusiastic organiser of activities and forever available to help individuals more severely disabled than himself.

In 1987 he was awarded the MBE, an honour indeed for a modest man who had overcome disability and had given consistent service to his fellow men.

Eddie Weldon was the orthotist selected to follow Bill Craddock. He too has continued to this day to deliver high quality service to the school.

Mr & Mrs Bill Craddock MBE.

The Holistic Vision

It was in the eighties that a seismic shift occurred. In the early seventies Margaret Barass, Head Physiotherapist, had investigated a holistic system of education for children and adults with motor disorders called Conductive Education or the Petó System. It had been designed and implemented in Budapest by Dr Andras Petó. This system advocated that children worked best in groups with 'conductors' whose extensive specialist training covered all aspects of a cerebral palsy child's needs and the appropriate solutions to meet them. It had appeal; but without trained conductors and such limited knowledge outside of Hungary it was difficult to implement. However, Margaret did set to work with one small group with Athetosis but this effort lacked serious support and could not be sustained for long. It was not until the BBC showed a film "Standing up for Joe" in 1987 that a serious interest in Conductive Education gathered momentum. Many parents with raised hopes strived to attend the Petó Institute Budapest at considerable cost in a desperate effort to have their cerebral palsy child upright and walking regardless of the degree of motor disfunction.

As early as 1965 one physiotherapist, Ester Cotton, visited the Petó Institute to seek out information and meet Professor Andras Petó.

Ester Cotton with her husband Bob.

Ester had worked with Dr and Mrs Bobath at their London centre as a senior tutor and at a later date became Physiotherapy Advisor to the Spastics Society. She was very impressed by what she observed and had continuous correspondence with Professor Pető up to the time of his death in 1967. From hereon she strived to introduce Conductive Education into the UK and abroad. She had the good fortune to work with a head teacher, Edna Varty (Thompson) of Ingfield Manor School, Sussex who had the foresight to see the advantages of this unique system. Together they were able to gain further knowledge and persuade the Spastics Society to build a purpose built Conductive Education Unit at Ingfield Manor as a model in 1976. They were successful in training a team comprised of teachers, therapists and nursery nurses to adopt the role of conductors. However, it was recognised that this was not ideal. It was clear that a trained conductor was not a mixture of professions but a single professional in their own right. Above all, it was recognised that this was an education system and not another treatment method and the ultimate achievement was not necessarily independent walking for every child. It meant varying degrees of achievement across all areas of development for each child. Also by a unification of philosophy, knowledge and effort time could be used economically. For the cerebral palsied child "time is their greatest enemy but can be their greatest asset".

Conductive Education was seen by the enlightened as very wide ranging, all-encompassing, not a rigid system but one which could be adapted and modified for many different groups and ages manifesting motor/neurological disorder, either congenital or acquired.

In the mid-seventies Edna Varty married and moved North and came to live near Hexham and applied for a teaching post in the infants' class at Percy Hedley. She was well-known and respected by David Johnston who welcomed her into the school but he had one stipulation – she was not to introduce Conductive Education into the class room and there was no evidence that her experience of this system influenced the established pattern of working at the time.

It was in 1979 that I became dissatisfied with the long term results of the treatment methods we had used for twenty years. Many adults whom I had known since their early childhood were living in Chipchase House or attending the workshop daily. Where skills and varying degrees of independence had been acquired in many instances they diminished or were not expected or encouraged therefore easily lost. Added to this I had felt for many years that the cerebral palsied child had a very fragmented school day due to the need for therapy sessions, clinical and psychological sessions of which all occurred episodically outside of the classroom. At the end of every summer term Heads of Departments, teachers and Head Teacher spent many hours constructing time tables for the following year. Each child's day was carved up and I was very conscious of the teacher's role and her responsibility for covering the curriculum and continuity of learning for the group. The adverse effect of constant interruptions by removing children from the classroom occupied my mind but I could not see a solution.

In her time Val Culloty had ensured that physiotherapists spent some time working in classrooms and she saw the advantages in group work in the gym. Outpatient pre-school groups became an accepted part of the therapists' role on Tuesday and Friday mornings, the aims being social, therapeutic and psychological.

The Friday group.

After expressing my feelings of dissatisfaction Dr Ellis suggested that I should visit Ingfield Manor School followed by Claremont School, Bristol where conductive education had been introduced. I was impressed by the practice in both but without understanding.

Whenever a staff member attended a course or encountered something new they were expected to give a short account of their observations at a full staff meeting at the end of Friday afternoon. On return I did this without any expectation of anything more than general interest being shown. When David Johnston said, "Why don't you do it?" and he really meant it I was incredulous. I did not know how to square up to such a challenge and I questioned whether he understood the upheaval the introduction of CE would cause throughout the school. However, I remembered Ester Cotton's advice "Do not attempt this unless the Head Teacher is right behind you". Undoubtedly he was and together with Dr Ellis, Heads of Departments and the Management Committee we moved on. Without that degree of inter-departmental cooperation, good will, enthusiasm and the established pioneering spirit, never would we have survived and thrived.

The effort, energy and support for this project had to be maintained against a background of hostility from factions far and wide who claimed that without recognised conductor training endorsed by The Peto Institute, Budapest, the practice was impure and distorted. Ester Cotton made valiant efforts to co-operate with The Peto Institute to design an appropriate training package for British teachers, therapists, doctors and nursery nurses which would provide a recognised qualification.

A group of eager early learners.

Meantime, short six week introductory courses in Budapest were made available and in the UK the Conductive Education Association was established. It attracted members both here and abroad and proved a valuable platform for communication, contacts, sharing of information and expansion of knowledge. Regular committee meetings and an annual AGM combined with a weekend course attracted many members. An informative journal was produced annually between 1986 and 1995.

Competition for recognition was in evidence throughout the eighties and this resulted in one project in particular; the selection of ten qualified British teachers to attend The Peto Institute for a three year CE training course interspersed with practise at the Birmingham Institute for CE which opened in 1986. This was followed in 1993 by a second major project supported by Scope whereby twelve young well qualified school leavers were accepted for training at The Peto Institute. On completion of the three year course they were destined to take up posts in Scope schools. Eventually this led on to establishing a recognised UK degree course at Keele University. Throughout this period and against a background of continuing controversy the Percy Hedley School and others continued to pursue their goal and thrive.

The first Conductive Education Class in 1982.

By 1980, when Conductive Education was introduced at Percy Hedley, there were a hundred and thirty children on the roll. The majority were below average intelligence, a minority were above. Almost half had speech, language and learning problems, the others had varying degrees of cerebral palsy. Twenty-eight children were weekly boarders. The catchment area stretched from the Cumbrian coast, north to the border and south to North Yorkshire. As well as teachers and care staff there were six physiotherapists, four occupational therapists and six speech therapists to attend to the needs of the children.

The first step required support and commitment from all quarters and once this was assured we were able to construct our strategy for implementation of practice. The planning took almost a year. It entailed education of staff, ordering new furniture, constructional alterations to the working area, installation of a viewing window and the formation of an inter-disciplinary team. As the nursery children would be joined by new admissions it was necessary to have discussions with all the parents about the new system. The children would be attending daily, therefore, the parents had a crucial role to play if the goals were to be achieved. No resistance was encountered in spite of the fact that all had grown accustomed to the usual practice of one-to-one communication with therapists and teacher. As function was meaningful to them the parents appeared to welcome a system which they readily understood and one in which they could usefully participate.

Anne Ferguson, infants teacher, conducting a sitting task series.

Children learning to sit upright, to look, listen and learn.

Learning to swim – Doreen Coxon, Susan Hall and Liz Potts.

The inter-disciplinary team consisted of the teacher and two nursery nurses who were constantly with the class. They were joined by a speech, occupational and physiotherapist on different days of the week. All agreed to work consistently together, plan appropriate programmes, learn the art of conducting and constantly change roles. A one week course was held in school for twenty-five staff. It included the chosen team, all therapists, the Deputy Head and three care staff. Ester Cotton supervised the training as well as advising on the organisation of the working area and the group to be conducted. The following week conductive education practice began.

All were very tense at this stage as they attempted to do everything correctly, nevertheless, the children responded very quickly to the new situation. Improved concentration was the first heartening observation. This encouraging response together with the enthusiasm which had been generated, helped everyone to persevere and surmount the hurdles. From the outset it was intended that the system should encompass the whole school day. Time after school, therefore, had to be used for programme planning and to formulate realistic goals for the group. It became evident that a further meeting, chaired by the Headmaster, each week was necessary. An

Jason and Lucy, just good friends.

agenda was presented which included items about policy and grievances (of which there were many at this stage). However, it had been agreed at the outset that all would persevere for three years. At that point an appraisal would indicate whether or not to continue or capitulate. At the end of three years no one wished to revert to previous practices. During the three year trial period there were a number of changes in practice as more knowledge was acquired: more short courses had been attended, more had been read, written and discussed. From time to time Ester Cotton returned to monitor progress and advise. There had been a marked change of attitude of staff and parents as emphasis shifted to this very positive approach i.e. concentrating on what a child can do rather than what he cannot do.

No account was taken at this point of a progression into the next class. This was planned a few weeks before the first clutch of nursery children had to move to the first infants class. They still had much more to learn and it was necessary to maintain the momentum. A second team of conductors was assembled who would operate a modified system which allowed more time for cognitive work. There were less specific programmes, but between times practice and reinforcement were in evidence. During the first hour of each day the integrated team could be seen assisting the children who were practising their newly acquired skills. Plinths were installed to provide the surface and fixation points to which the children were already accustomed. A standing and walking programme and a writing programme were incorporated in the timetable. All opportunities were used to practise skill transfer and to reinforce what had been learnt. It was not until stage two was reached that the questions "But where is the education?" stopped being asked. It had been of some concern from the outset by some, teachers in particular, that the initial emphasis on improved motor performance would interfere with the nursery curriculum. How would it be incorporated in the programmes? Would there be enough time to encompass everything? Such questions were understandable. The physical content of the system tends to mask the subtle introduction of nursery curriculum content. It emerged in "Infants One" that the children were concentrating well and that they had absorbed the basic nursery education. There were no behaviour problems and they appeared to be contented with their school day. Parents' enthusiasm and co-operation had not wavered after five years. On the occasions when they had been invited to attend for any reason, very rarely had a child been unrepresented.

Stage three was launched. Some of the children were about to progress to the first Junior class. Another inter-disciplinary team had to be formed. In 1986 a junior teacher altered the rhythm of the school day in order to perpetuate the system. She concentrated on further functional progress where possible and put emphasis on establishment of skills already achieved. She had spent some time observing them in the infants group and had familiarised herself with the system.

Helen Jackson was the Head Occupational Therapist and, apart from her professional skills, she had excellent artistic and creative ability which proved a bonus in this setting for team members and children alike. In 1986 she attended the first six week course for English speakers at The Peto Institute in Budapest. It was emphasised that this was an introduction and observation exercise only and did not qualify anyone for conductor status. On return her recommendations were implemented and they included an extension of the working area in the reception class to accommodate more children who were being referred. These courses were repeated and I followed on.

Throughout this period there was a nagging problem. We had no objective assessment to act as a basis for acceptable evaluation in the prevailing climate of hostility, media publicity, limited training and limited literature. Those of us who had been involved with cerebral palsied children for many years could only claim, both in the practice of the system and the outcome, subjectively that there was substantial improvement. This manifested itself in different ways: a unity of effort by team members with a clear sense of direction. The school day was used economically with far fewer classroom interruptions. Team members with particular creative or musical abilities influenced those less able and ignited dormant talents which gave opportunities for expression and improvement. We had in our midst team members who had no professional qualifications who over time acquired skills, theoretical knowledge and above all practice. They had particular personalities best suited for team work and related well with children, parents and colleagues.

The children showed enthusiasm for improving their performance functionally. Improved concentration and stamina were in evidence. As a group they became more socially aware which in turn resulted in a willingness to co-

The Team for Infants 2. Jill Collerton, Judith Kirkland, Maureen Summers, Helen Jackson, Catherine Baines, Karol Lalor and Margaret Donkin.

operate, compete, strive and take pride in their performance. Those who worked together throughout that exciting five year period were able to reflect on a system that developed slowly, gathered momentum, and eventually became infectious in the school. The fundamental principles and practice of CE were addressed but the style and shape were individual and peculiar to the setting in which it was developed. The mutual transition in 1981 required careful planning and the practice in the first two years was painful at times. Continuation and transference into an increasing number of older groups proved easier.

Throughout this period David Johnston monitored progress and gave full support to the implementation of an education system which generated so much interest without and so much enthusiasm within. Likewise, Professor Donald Court took a keen interest and spent time observing the work, giving positive advice and encouragement. It was recognised that there would be overwhelming advantages in early referral and group work in a School for Parents and this realistic vision became a reality in 2003 led by Head Physiotherapist, Anne Coates, and her chosen partner was Doreen Coxon who had been employed initially as a classroom assistant and demonstrated a natural aptitude for this role.

David Johnston retired in 1985 and there were those of us who feared that his successor might not be familiar with CE or have any desire to perpetuate it. Once he was appointed Rosemary Pattison (Deputy Head Teacher) and I gathered various papers which were sent to him in Northern Ireland in advance of him taking up his post. We had underestimated our man.

Jim Ferris in fact raised the stakes and recognised that what had already been achieved was more than worthy of perpetuation, expansion and full support. His consistent involvement throughout his headship resulted in continued expansion and refinement within school to a point where it was necessary to appoint a Head of Conductive Education. Hazel Howliston, a Junior Teacher, was well qualified for this role. She had an excellent track record and was the leader of her CE team. Also, she had visited and worked for three weeks with two other staff members and a group of Percy Hedley children and their parents in Budapest in 1988 at the invitation of the Director of the Peto Institute, Dr Maria Hari.

Jim Ferris.

Within a short time Jim Ferris became well known to those in the UK who were pioneering the CE system. He was actively involved in the CE Association and played a key role in the pursuit of acceptable training for Percy Hedley staff members. While recognising the shortfall and the complexities of transferring a system from one culture to another he skilfully circumvented the continuing arguments by re-naming our practice 'Integrated Education'. He was responsible for placing requests to the Management Committee for financial support for selected individuals to attend courses in Budapest, to visit other centres and attend the CE Association AGM. I do not recollect there being any refusals. Over time all Heads of Departments were given this valuable opportunity.

Grasping the Future
Tyne Tees Film 1988

In the early 1980s there was much controversy surrounding the system of Conductive Education. The Percy Hedley School was at the heart of this. Owing to media publicity parents of cerebral palsied children, desperate for a solution made great sacrifices to travel to the Peto Institute, Budapest. The Percy Hedley School, working against this tide had begun to satisfy the demand for a system based on knowledge of Conductive Education. Publicity was necessary to draw attention to the local effort and to inject realism into what was rapidly becoming an 'hysteria'.

As Head of Physiotherapy, I approached a neighbour, Mr John Reay, who was a producer at Tyne Tees TV and asked him how to set about planning and constructing a documentary film. The first task was to provide a brief synopsis of the aims, the content and the message to be broadcast. This would be set before a panel responsible for selecting topics from a list which are considered worthy of production. This particular hurdle was overcome and filming was organised by a private company based in Stowell Street, Newcastle and the producer, Roy Deane, came from Tyne Tees. We worked together filming over three days and it was quite remarkable how well the children, some individually and some in groups, worked and were not distracted by all the equipment and two unknown men in their classroom.

Tyne Tees Film Crew.

This film was shown at 10.35 pm on Thursday, 28th April 1988 and it proved a success. It was presented in October 1990 at the John Muir Medical Festival in San Francisco where it competed against six hundred entries to win a Gold Award in the Pro/Rehabilitation category. Festival Director, Chip Bissell, said of the programme, "It joins an elite group of the finest productions available today".

A good relationship had been built up with the production team and so it was two years later that I approached them again for help to produce a training video. It was explained how this could be done and the costs involved which ranged from £4,000 – £50,000 for film length of thirty-five minutes and that production of less than five hundred copies would not be cost effective. Having investigated what we might get for £4,000 and being satisfied, an approach was made by Jim Ferris to the Management Committee for funding. This was granted and we repeated the film procedure but this time we had greater responsibility for script writing, selection of shots, the title and designing the cover.

Hazel Howliston, class teacher in Junior 1 and I spent many hours on this task. It also involved visits to the film studio in Stowell Street to work through nine reels of film to select the best shots to match the script for a thirty-five minute video film. Finally, we had to select a reader with moderate pace and a voice which would be easy on the ear. Rosemary Pattison, Deputy Headteacher, had the necessary qualities for this role.

Over the following ten years this film proved a useful teaching aid within schools in the UK and abroad. Copies were sold to parents and other institutions. In Poland the script was translated and used widely. It sold well.

At the time the granting of funding for this film by the Management Committee was greatly appreciated. Although there were no conditions attached to this agreement we felt we should make every effort to recoup some of the outlay, and this was achieved.

LEARNING
FOR
LIVING

"I sit ready to
Look, Listen, and Learn"

Care Staff

Success depended on co-operation from all quarters at all levels. Not least of these were care staff who were responsible for twenty-eight weekly boarders in 1980. Being in loco parentis their contribution was essential for providing time and opportunity for children to practice newly learnt skills. The changes which had taken place over the years did not always run smoothly in this department and this is understandable when the history is examined.

Anne Christer (McGuire) was twelve years old when the school opened in 1953. At that time she had joined the Red Cross Cadets and a call went out for volunteers to help the Percy Hedley children in the evenings. Anne and two others responded but it was not until she was eighteen that she was able to apply for a full-time post as a Housemother and her starting salary was £7.50 a month.

Although she lived locally she was in residence for the first few weeks of employment and worked from 7.30 am to 7.00 pm with occasional breaks during the day. Each Housemother was responsible for four or five children known as her 'family'.

When her family were in class there were other duties requiring attention and going into the laundry room was one. It was uninviting, located at the north west corner of the building as far away as possible from 'Firtrees'. It was cold in summer and arctic in winter. The machine was a mighty juggernaut and drying

Anne Christer (McGuire).

facilities were limited. On fine days a small secluded garden at the back proved a blessing. There it was possible to hang out washing without causing offence to passers by.

Apart from a six month maternity break Anne was employed at the Percy Hedley Centre until her retirement as Head of Care in 2006. Miss Grainger, who was appointed as the first matron, started on 1st January 1953 and was described as "a wonderfully motherly little lady". She was then succeeded by Miss Black. There were no recognised courses available for care staff at that time so new recruits had to follow Matron's strict rules and regulations. For them this was a journey of discovery.

There were two Assistant Matrons who slept in and acted as night staff. All were housed in Hampeth Lodge. Miss Black was afforded the privilege of Jenny Pearson as her personal maid who attended to her every need. After a few years of scurrying to and from the kitchen with a tea tray, eventually Jenny escaped this life of 'servitude' and became a Housemother.

Miss Black's rules included embroidering 'PHS' on all the towels, daily inspections of dormitories, the beds, the lockers and equipment. There were no lifts or hoists so children had to be carried up and down between floors.

There existed something of a power struggle in these early years between Matron and Headteacher. One insisted on silence at all times in the corridors, the other disagreed and these minor differences spilled over into other areas of daily management.

In 1959 a second boarding house 'Firtrees' was ready to accommodate a further twenty-four children in four rooms with six children in each. It was a traumatic day when twenty new boarders arrived together. Parting from parents, home sickness, a new environment and new carers contributed to a period of distress. Eventually the situation was resolved and to this day there are some of those children who remain in regular contact with staff members who

Firtrees House.

have since retired. There were many examples of sound relationships with long-serving staff members in all departments which have survived the years. Linda McMahon, one of the first children to attend the school, lives in the Alston area and until his death she corresponded with and visited David Johnston regularly.

After school hours and over the weekends resident children played and were entertained by care staff. Until a school bus or qualified drivers emerged the children remained mainly in the school precinct, although there were occasions when the owner of Chipchase House invited children to play in the grounds. This was just across the main road from the school and it was here that they enjoyed picnics, playing in long grass and looking at the stream which flowed towards the culvert under the main road.

Without a school bus outings were confined to walks in the vicinity. Black's Paper Shop, situated at the entrance to Benton Station, was a particular attraction. Two brothers, the owners, came to know all the local children very well over many years and they made genuine effort to accommodate the Percy Hedley children who had to be assisted out of their wheelchairs into the shop. The step was too high. There was no ramp and walkways were too narrow for a wheelchair. In their way, the brothers Black contributed positively to the integration of the disabled into their local community. In appreciation of their valuable contribution Mr and Mrs S Black were invited into school for coffee and a guided tour. Just a

Presentation of a new mini bus.

mention of their names today to adults in Chipchase House and they are well remembered for their style that was perpetuated until the shop's closure in 2009

When a local firm donated a second hand ambulance and a parent volunteered to drive, the children were able to go into the countryside and to the beach.

Between 1.00 – 1.30 pm the children had to lie down and rest on folding camp beds and in the evening they were made ready for bed by six o'clock in order to fit the work schedule of the carers. Although this rigid regime may appear harsh today it should be remembered that many of these children had been deprived of opportunities for social interaction beyond their homes. Here they were learning to play, to communicate and make friends. The staff were young and inexperienced so they too had much to learn by way of child care, management, structure, communication with parents and cerebral palsy. They had to learn to be observant, sensitive and responsive in an emergency.

Epilepsy is recognised as one of a number of problems associated with cerebral palsy. In the fifties, although monitoring and anticonvulsive medication were available, they lacked the sophistication of the present day. As a result those children who were susceptible had frequent episodes and for the inexperienced carer this could prove alarming. However, Dr Ellis contributed greatly to the understanding of this condition as well as injecting confidence in the management of children when they became sick. His list of clear instructions was aimed at reducing panic reactions. The list for those children requiring a speedy response was short therefore easy to remember: - convulsions, excessive bleeding from any source, severe abdominal pain and earache.

Changes in the work place are frequently received with suspicion, rejection, reluctance or even downright obstruction on occasions. Without well considered changes over time the Percy Hedley Foundation would not be able to record the progress made to date. David Johnston, once appointed as headteacher, regarded the care system with dismay as being Dickensian, unimaginative and stagnant. He was well acquainted with residential care from previous experience as deputy headteacher at Netherton Approved School near Morpeth and his aims were to make life for the day and residential child more palatable, more exciting and to widen their experience of this world as it is. The changes which he initiated were not well received initially and a period of much grumbling ensued. However, with patience, persistence and above all by example he achieved his goal. From the outset David Johnston was involved directly with the children, the teachers and carers on a daily basis. A headteacher's house had been purchased for him and his family at 21 Station Road, right beside the school. He was available for care staff to call him in for any emergency. His three young teenage sons spent many hours with the children in leisure time, on weekend trips and camping holidays. Gone were the days of the matron and no housemother was senior to any other. No uniforms were worn either. By 1964 there were forty-four resident children and a team of nine housemothers to look after them, each with a 'family' of four or five children to care for. The team approach was emphasised which involved frequent staff meetings to discuss residential issues and if any supervision was required it was exercised by the headteacher or his deputy. The duty of the housemother was to address all the daily needs of the child; to be involved in their therapy and their classroom, to keep in close contact with their family and if necessary to pay home visits.

During the school day there were other duties to perform; assisting in therapy at meal times and in school breaks. There never was and never are enough helping hands for children with special needs. In 1971 when there were ninety-two children attending school an increased recruitment of staff was not an option because an economy drive was being imposed upon them at the time.

David Johnston had already broken the mould by introducing the split shift system for care staff which was not readily accepted. Too much too soon would have ignited the 'what next' factor but he recognised a real need to get a man around the house. There were few men employed in the building and those who were, were not in regular contact with the children. Tom and Fred were general maintenance, at service to everyone needing a job done. Gordon Crowther was chief administrator, Dr Ellis was fully employed with clinical duties and all therapists were female.

Against this background David Johnston introduced a system of employment for Community Service Volunteers. He appealed to the recognised CSV organisation for a young, male school leaver who needed to fill a gap year. This proved to be a great idea. For the care staff a young lad living away from home would not present a threat. They could train him, mould him and he would be that extra pair of hands that they craved and so it was that at the start of each winter term a new interesting lad would join the staff. A few did not last out the year but for the majority it was a valuable experience and for one in particular it was both valuable and memorable.

Steve Thompson was one such volunteer. He lived with his parents and sister in Mexborough and until he was sixteen years old he had the ambition to pursue a career in music. When he failed the Grade 8 piano exam he was daunted and his enthusiasm waned. He went on to a sixth form college but by the final year he had no real sense of direction. Quite by chance he came upon an advertisement about Community Service Volunteers which had appeal. He was eager to leave home so he applied and presented himself for interview in London. He had to sign an agreement to go wherever he was sent and on this occasion it was to be Reading where the remit was to undertake supervised social work. Steve was all set for Reading until he received a call informing him of a change of plan only two days before departure. "You are needed in Newcastle upon Tyne on Monday". He could not make it by Monday so he had to ring the Headteacher, David Johnston, for an extra day to prepare himself. Steve had little idea of North East geography so had to refer to a map to find his destination.

On Tuesday, 4 September 1971 Steve Thompson set off for Newcastle. It was his first journey North and the first time he had lived away from home. In all his eighteen years he had only ever encountered one wheelchair bound child, known to have unacceptable behaviour problems and as for cerebral palsy, it was quite unknown to him.

He caught the Tynerider from Newcastle Central Station (the Metro system came later) and got off at Benton. It was a lovely evening and the surrounding trees were still in leaf and with a suitcase in each hand he set forth from Black's Newsagents down the path to the T-junction. As he walked he could identify the school building ahead and soon he became aware of the noisy, happy voices of children playing in the grounds. At this point he became terrified and this terror mounted when he espied them racing round in wheelchairs. His initial reaction almost convinced him that he would not be able to do the job.

However, he received a warm welcome and was given a small, single room in Firtrees, full board and a salary of £2.50 per week plus rail fares home for holidays. The care team accepted him and did his laundry and ironing. In spite of his youthful wish to leave home he did have a tinge of homesickness in the first few weeks. Now; Steve was a people person. He could make friends easily, the children liked him from day one, he played football and he was a good pianist. There was only one thing missing. Steve could not swim but that was soon rectified when Gary Dixon taught him.

Steve Thompson on the beach with David in 1972.

Gary had cerebral palsy but was fairly ambulant. Once into his stride Steve made a number of trips away with children. On one occasion he accompanied Raymond O'Dowd, a senior teacher and Fred Lapsley, driver and general maintenance man, on a week long trip to Scotland where he was given responsibility for pushing David Cairns in his wheelchair round the Isle of Bute. On some evenings he played football with boys in the gym. In fine weather, football was played in the courtyard where they were sometimes joined by some local lads. At the time Steve noticed one ten year old who lived in Victoria Avenue, Forest Hall – a street adjoining the school – who demonstrated footwork and ball skills well beyond his years. His name was Peter Beardsley, who eventually became famous as a Newcastle United player.

Steve left the school in July 1972, the staff were sorry to see him go, moreso the children. As a parting gift one boy, David Foreshaw, known to his friends as Budgie, insisted on giving him the gold medal which he had received after competing in a national sporting event at Stoke Mandeville. That medal remains, to this day, as one of Steve's treasures.

After the gap year Steve Thompson tried psychiatric nursing for one year but this was not for him. Only after a spell as a fishmonger and one or two delivery jobs all in the area did he settle for a teaching career and married life in the North East.

Peter Beardsley signs autographs on the day he presented a new Sunshine Coach.

In 2010, at the age of fifty-seven Steve is teaching at Ravenswood School, Heaton where he has particular responsibility for IT programmes and music.

Until the arrival of Denis Mundy in 1990 there had not been a man fully employed as a 'housefather' in school. When Denis was in his mid-thirties he decided to embark on a National Nursery Examination Board course because he had always wanted to work with children. Places on the course in 1988 were limited and there was a four month wait before his place was confirmed. On the first day he discovered he was the only man in an intake of fifty participants which to him was something of a shock. Furthermore they were aged twenty one and under and he was a married man with

Denis Mundy helping to run the boys' club.

children. The two year course included both practical and written work. This included Health & Social Studies, Communication and Social Skills, Physical Education and Home Economics. The practical placements covered first schools, nursery schools, special schools and hospitals. His two week placement in Senior I class at the Percy Hedley School in 1989 was like no other and he approached it with some degree of trepidation. The class teacher, Trish Rose, introduced him to a system of working with children he had never encountered before. Staff members were sympathetic and in the midst of their tight schedules found time to teach on the hoof and answer his endless string of questions.

At the end of the second year he applied for a post as a 'housefather'. He claimed to be very, very nervous when he attended for interview but was overjoyed when he learnt that he had been successful. His forty nine young female fellow students were genuinely thrilled for him too because they were aware of his enthusiasm to work in that place.

By 1986 all resident children returned home every weekend. Although his key role was the care and well-being of these children, Denis was involved with work in the class

House mothers. Back row: Miss Moat, Anne Christer, Kathy Nicholson, Elsie Watson, Katherine Armstrong. Front: Mrs Craggs, Elsie Ferguson, Suzette Ridley, Jenny Pearson & Jenny Ferguson.

rooms too. Over and above a recognised training in any discipline this special environment opens up endless opportunities for the exposure and utilisation of individual natural talent. This has untold benefits for the children, for colleagues and for one's self esteem. Many employees are remembered for their particular creative ability; their musicality, their comedy, their artistic creations and sporting ability. Denis was involved in the Young Ornithologists' Group and the Sports Clubs.

Evening and weekend leisure activities were in the hands of some very willing teachers and therapists. As well as Scouts, Guides, Cubs and Brownie meetings, there was an Art Club, a Photography Group, a games night and a group who visited an outside swimming pool.

Some of the older children joined outside youth clubs while several more found a hobby in breeding pigeons. There were a few who were too disabled to be involved usefully in these activities. For some this was frustrating but others were content to be spectators.

The accepted practice was for therapists to advise on and demonstrate lifting and handling techniques, particular therapeutic exercises to be practised and general management of individual children. However, it proved extremely difficult to convince carers, class teachers and parents that divorcing therapy from every other aspect of the child's daily life was uneconomical and non-productive. Account had to be taken of the time and effort required to fit in all the demands being made upon then. It does well to remember there were no serious 'lifting and handling' courses available, or special hoists and for parents living in poor social conditions with large families this could prove taxing.

A real and lasting change in attitude came about from 1980 onwards when the total holistic education system was introduced in the school. Anne McGuire (formerly Christer) had married and her daughter was born in 1969. She relinquished her post for six months' maternity leave and allowances were not an option in 1969. The care staff were operating a split shift system of duties which was not compatible with the role of wife and mother so Anne returned to work as a physiotherapy aide and remained in this post for seventeen years before transferring back to her original role of housemother. This move had some very positive benefits. Anne had worked alongside therapists and learnt much more about cerebral palsy, about treatment methods and the importance of fostering practice of new skills as well as providing opportunities for these skills to be generalised. She was the ideal 'go-between' and her influence ignited a change in understanding, in practice and attitudes. Moreover, she had had the opportunity to participate in the first conductive education course held in school in 1980. There was a transfer of knowledge and philosophy.

"What better example of child care could you find than that achieved by our housemothers and in particular Anne Christer. I remember Anne Christer as a Red Cross Cadet almost at the beginning of the Percy Hedley School cleaning children's shoes, but I shall never forget her devoted care of John Metcalf, one of the most severely disabled children that I have ever seen. I have a very clear picture of Ann in the bottom sick room holding a desperately ill little boy in her arms right up to the time that I had to take him into Walkergate Hospital, where he died a few hours later".

Dr Errington Ellis, 1969

Anne McGuire with residents Margaret McHugh And Margaret Caines.

Speech and Language Therapy

One Speech Therapist, Enid Taylor (1953-58), was employed in school in 1953 when the focus was on feeding, swallowing and articulation problems associated with cerebral palsy. In 2010 she remembers her early days at the Percy Hedley Centre.

"When I arrived at the Percy Hedley Centre in March 1953 I little realised that I was taking part in an exciting new venture. The whole place had an air of expectancy that great things were going to happen in the treatment of cerebral palsied children. The Director of the centre was a young paediatrician called Dr Errington Ellis who had the charisma, the tenacity and the charm to make his staff believe that miracles were possible.

However on the day that I arrived, the centre consisted of Hampeth Lodge, a Victorian house of moderate proportions and a new school building. The stables of the Lodge were still under construction as treatment rooms. The one physiotherapist was a delightful lady from Southern Ireland with the imposing name of Honoria Valentine Culloty, known to her friends as Val. She had already had three month's training with Dr Karl Bobath and his wife Berta who had devised a new way of treating cerebral palsied children. Val had the laborious task of explaining this new method to me which was quite foreign to a speech therapist.

Since there were no clinical rooms we worked in the children's bedrooms on large wooden tables specially made for the treatment. From the beginning we liaised closely with the teachers in the school. The headteacher, Molly Cauldwell, was a lady with boundless energy, great kindness and a flair for organising second to none.

Therapy staff were encouraged to take part in school outings (the physio staff had now risen to three – Marjorie Raine and Maureen Townsend now assisting Val).

We helped to carry children miles across Bamburgh sands to find just the right spot for a picnic. We indulged in the fairyland of the theatre in the Round, and on one never to be forgotten trip we went to the circus sitting in specially selected seats as near to the ring as possible and an elephant wishing to be sociable no doubt, decided he would relieve himself as near to us as he could get causing roars of laughter from the audience as the waterfall descended on us.

Molly Cauldwell also decided that the staff should entertain the children at Christmas and I was dragooned into arranging it. However, there was a major problem in that the 'performers' were always so busy it was almost impossible to arrange any rehearsals. We did manage to put on an almost perfect 'Cinderella' – just as well as the Press attended but the following shows 'Snow White and the Seven Dwarfs' and 'Goldilocks and the Three Bears' relied tremendously on Hilda Shield, the deputy headteacher, and an accomplished pianist, to improvise when words were forgotten or characters failed to appear.

As the fame of the centre spread there became a pressing need for a unit with facilities for children and parents to stay for several nights to be fully assessed. Money for the unit came from many sources but primarily from Newcastle University's annual Rag Week. In order to advertise the Appeal students made an extremely good film of the work of the centre which was shown in all the cinemas in the Newcastle area. It was a very strange sensation to see oneself on the big screen.

Probably the highlight of my time at Percy Hedley was the day that HRH Princess Marina, formerly the Duchess of Kent, opened the centre. I have a recollection of a most beautiful bouquet lying on a table waiting for the presentation, the smell

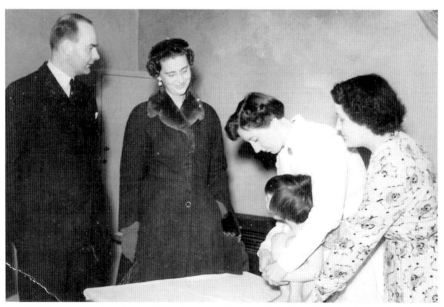

Dr Ellis escorting The Duchess of Kent with Val Cullotty and Sadie Mckenzie.

of white freesias perfuming the air. The Duchess was the epitome of graciousness and we all managed to perform our curtsies without falling over while Dr Ellis looked on with amusement. He, of course, performed his role with superb aplomb.

My days at the Percy Hedley Centre were certainly rewarding. Perhaps the nicest part has been the people I met who continued to be friends long after I had left the centre."

In line with the pupil population the number of speech therapists grew and the focus was on children with cerebral palsy who had specific speech problems.

In 1957 one child who was not diagnosed with cerebral palsy but with a degree of movement abnormality was admitted to the school. He had a speech and language disorder. By 1962 seven more children so diagnosed had been admitted. This was a period of growing awareness of speech and language disorders in children and it highlighted a lack of

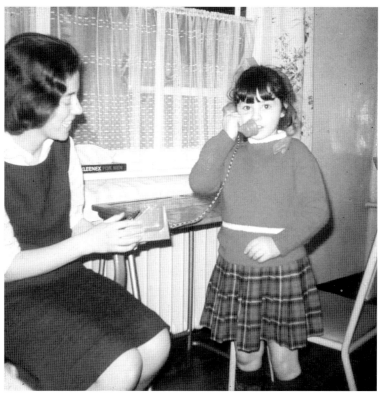

Learning to communicate.

Rosemary Pattison, Deputy Headteacher, and Margaret Ashford, Senior Language Teacher.

provision of specialised education in the Northern region. The recognition of this problem coincided with a secondary problem relating to the reduction in referrals of cerebral palsied children from some local authorities whose budgets limited the availability of fees. This was an opportunity to address these burning issues so by 1962 there were seven children with these problems who were in small classes alongside those with cerebral palsy. From 1963 onwards the numbers increased substantially and the school inspectors advocated a change of policy which was to separate the two categories as their needs were quite different. In September 1968 the first class of six children with specific speech and language disorders was opened. They ranged in age from five – ten years and the average stay in the class was five terms. The majority remained at the Percy Hedley School until the official leaving age, while others moved on elsewhere. By 1970 it was clear that a senior language class would be necessary and this became a reality by 1975. There were by this time one hundred and twenty-seven pupils on roll and twenty-nine of those had receptive language disorders. By 1981 a second junior class was created. Each class had a specialist language teacher and classroom assistant. These changes were gathering momentum at the same time as the Integrated Education system was taking effect and there was genuine commitment to it.

This called for a review of the Primary Department and it became apparent that the younger children with speech and language disorders needed separate educational provision. The first infant language class opened in 1984. For some children sign language was essential for communication. It had been introduced originally for two children whose speech was unintelligible but were able to learn and understand the complexities of the English language. Paget Gorman Signed Speech was considered to be the most appropriate system for Percy Hedley children because it gave full range of expression. This breakthrough resulted in a reduction of frustration, an improved attitude to learning leading on to improvement in reading and writing. To be successful a supplementary method of communication has to involve all who have daily contact with the child; parents, pupil and staff. To achieve this an open forum was held on 10 June 1986 to describe alternative methods and to encourage staff and parents to learn signing. Classes for this purpose were arranged and tutored by Lynne Birrell and senior language teacher, Margaret Ashford. It did not prove easy but we persevered.

Staff and pupils in the Senior Language Class, July 1989. Back row, left to right, Elliot Milburn, Brian Geldart, Michael Rain, Ian Wyre (CSV), Nigel Coulter, Michael Cameron. Front row, left to right, Joan Baker, Louise Moon, Lynne Birrell, Louise Taylor, Margaret Ashford, Angela Barlow.

By 1990 the number of language classes had increased to six for a total of fifty children. Speech therapists worked alongside teachers in the classroom and were supported by occupational therapists and physiotherapists who focused their attention on motor, co-ordination and organisational problems which affect these children to varying degrees. Lynne Birrell, Chief Speech Therapist and Jennifer Buckle, Head of Language Department were the prime movers in the development of this expanding service. They worked together to design and develop an appropriate curriculum. They made valuable contacts in the UK which enabled staff to benefit from a variety of courses, exchange visits and experiences. Up to 1990 the focus had been on creation of new language classes from thereon came the question of geographical location. The classes were scattered and did not make for easy management. After considerable upheaval and reconstruction over the summer holiday of 1990 the language classes could be located in one compact area,

All therapists have their particular preferences of how and where they work. In the centre there were those who preferred the Integrated Education Department and those who devoted their attention to the Language Department. Heads of Department respected such preferences as far as it was managerially possible, recognising that with some degree of choice, improved performance and results would ensue.

Pauline Adair, Senior Physiotherapist had a real and lasting interest in group work in the gym, in dance, in drama and athletics. Initially, she had to make use of one end of the dining hall. Following construction of a new gymnasium she was able to select appropriate equipment and set about designing programmes and progressions for many different groups both cerebral palsied and language disordered which were exciting and motivating. Regarding the latter group, Pauline was the one physiotherapist who worked most closely with Lynne and Jennifer to coordinate their curriculum content with her programmes thus ensuing that movement, language and function were intertwined.

The eighties could be described as the period of disciplinary fusion. It was 'Team Time' and involvement of the Occupational and Speech Therapists in the classroom was essential. Who they were, where they came from and their ultimate contribution resulted over time in a unity which provided an improved service for children and families.

Occupational Therapy

The school, the speech and physiotherapy departments had been in existence since 1953 so it was eighteen years before Rosemary Harvey, an experienced Occupational Therapist, presented herself and put forward a very strong case for this service.

Responsibility for ordering wheelchairs, equipment, checking and adapting tricycles had, up to 1971, lain with the physiotherapists. Either due to financial restrictions or ignorance of the role Occupational Therapy had been resisted. Whenever the subject arose it always prompted the question, "But what will they do?" What 'they' actually did once they arrived was welcomed. Physiotherapists were particularly pleased to relinquish their responsibility for 'trikes, bikes and other bits' but had little idea what might follow or be added. Once across the threshold Rosemary Harvey (Jenkins) assessed dining room seating and it was not long before she was reducing table heights and matching individual children appropriately. Working solo in a new role against established practices was not easy. It required determination and resilience and it was strength of character and style which carried her through. Unfortunately her reign was short lived because she married and moved on in 1971 just six months after the arrival of her basic inexperienced assistant, Helen Jackson.

Helen Jackson was born in Gatley, Cheshire in 1936. She was educated at Cheadle Hulme school. Here she met her future husband, Peter, who she married in 1959.

She trained as an Occupational Therapist at Dorset House, Oxford and following qualification she worked at Parkside Psychiatric Hospital, Macclesfield.

Following her marriage in 1959 she moved to Caithness where her husband was employed as a Research Metallurgist at Dounreay. Stationed there were many young families and Helen needed a job so she wrote to the Director of Education and was invited for an interview. She was offered the task of teaching twelve problem children of various ages; two were from the local Romany community who eventually excelled themselves. All were housed in an uninviting classroom. Without teaching qualifications and experience she had to acquire skills by trial and error but one teacher in particular offered valuable support over her two year period in the school. After which Helen had two sons to care for before

Helen Jackson working in the class room.

moving on to Derby in 1964. By 1971, now with three children, the family moved to Whitley Bay where her husband took up a post in the Parsons Industrial Research and Development department.

During that period they watched a documentary film about the Percy Hedley School which was part of a series about the North East, directed by Roger Burgess, a school contemporary. This was their main reason for watching it. Helen noted that two Occupational Therapists were working there: Rosemary Harvey and Marilyn Drummond. This was the first time she had been made aware that Occupational Therapists had a role in Special Education. It was viewed and forgotten until fourteen years on when her children were in full time education and with limited professional experience Helen looked for work. She had not opened her professional journal for years. She noted a vacancy for a basic grade post at the Percy Hedley School and it was then that she recalled the TV documentary programme. It required courage to apply for the post and when invited for interview apprehension took over and she did not expect success as she was not the sole applicant. Dr Ellis, Mr David Johnston and Mrs Rosemary Harvey were on the interview panel. Her CV included her unusual teaching experience in Caithness and this carried weight together with her experience as a mother of three. The panel were most interested in her knowledge about children.

The Occupational Therapy staff, 1993. Back row, left to right, Helen Jones, Stewart Evans, Carol Pyle. Front row, left to right, Helen Jackson, Ellen Errington, Linda Shaw.

Anna Nicholson working on an enlarged keyboard.

The problems of childcare were raised and she was asked about her plan. Dr Ellis pointed out "We would not want you if you did not put your own children first". It was pointed out that in the event of a child being sick, if necessary one should stay at home and relinquish pay.

Helen started work in September 1971 and within six months Rosemary Harvey moved on and could not be replaced due to financial strictures at that time. The situation proved daunting and she was indeed fearful. To allay her fears Dr Ellis instructed her to find her feet and make what she could of this department and develop it. She attended courses, learnt from home visiting and developed home plans as well as being supported by other staff members. Helen worked solo for three years before another post could be filled by Kathryn Turnbull. Kathryn played a key role in developing the integrated education system from the outset. In order to devote much more time to this aspect of the work Helen relinquished her role as Head Occupational Therapist and exchanged her position with Kathryn. There was some opposition to the idea but it worked out well. The 1970s was a time when Occupational Therapists focused attention on improving methods of written communication for children who were unable to use an electric typewriter with a keyboard in the classroom. The Possum expanded keyboard which had an enlarged keyboard with large letters was being introduced to

Ryan with his teacher Brenda Roberts learning to communicate via the computer.

some of the youngest children in preparation for simple word building and reading. The greatest challenge to teachers and therapists was a small group of children who could comprehend information but were unable to express themselves by conventional methods or through speech. Until a suitable method was found teachers were unable to ascertain how many concepts being taught were understood and retained. The solution was the introduction of remotely controlled electronic typewriters, either Possum or Electraid. After a detailed assessment a method of operation was reached. This entailed identification of a body part with the greatest degree of voluntary control. Once this was established these children needed daily individual sessions to learn how to control, operate and use the system before they could operate independently in the classroom. The therapists worked in conjunction with the Medical Physics Department of Newcastle University to reach the most satisfactory solution for each individual problem. Mr Gordon Flanagan, a lecturer in Medical Physics from that department became the first to advise and assist in training in Information Technology.

By 1980 the computer age was upon us and five Apple 2 personal computers had been acquired. These advances have opened up once unimagined opportunities for severely disabled children and the Percy Hedley therapists have moved with the times.

Helen Jackson did indeed develop that department and set in motion new initiatives which resulted in a quality service. Her experience combined with innate creative ability placed her in a key position to pursue the next pioneering route – the introduction of the integrated education programme and in 1985 she was the first Percy Hedley staff member to attend a six week introductory course on Conductive Education in Budapest.

Once established in the new role she developed writing programmes, songs and rhymes all of which were meticulously recorded in large volumes to which all staff had access. Working as a team member alongside her, one could not fail to be infected by her creativity and professional contribution.

Services for Adolescents and Adults

Success in one area at any time is sure to reveal the need for expansion and further effort. The children were receiving education up to sixteen years for what? A minority would seek outside employment, or further education, although such facilities were limited. The majority would have to return home to parents who were getting older unless their needs were addressed. Already, there were many adults with cerebral palsy of normal intelligence who were home-bound, unemployable and without interests outside their own homes. Many were leading lonely and frustrated lives and had become a burden to themselves and their families.

To help these people a Social Club was started at the Percy Hedley School in 1956. Transport, provided by Local Authorities, enabled the club to meet on one evening each week. Because of the lack of suitable facilities few of the club members had attended school, and the companionship of the club was the first that they had known outside their own family circle. The club helped them to make a better adjustment to life, and they were soon able to take a share in running the club and making their own entertainment. Their first venture was the formation of a drama group. At the time the Drama Advisor to the Institute of Education at Durham University was looking for a "different group" to produce and, with their help, the drama group produced a most successful Christmas play.

A handicraft class was also started. The benefits which resulted from these activities were out of all proportion to the simple facilities provided.

By 1958 these activities were expanded into a day workroom which was opened in a hut leased for a nominal rent by the Air Ministry on the RAF Balloon Barrage site, Whitley Road, Benton. This is now occupied by the Ministry of Pensions. Here the most heavily handicapped club members were able to experiment with simple outwork from local firms. Their first job was packing samples for Proctor and Gamble for their launch of Camay soap. Mr John Hodgson, an engineer, was appointed to supervise and develop this facility. When it became known locally that this workshop was able to respond to simple requests they did attract some odd customers from time to time. One such request came from a young mother seeking child care who wanted to park the pram for an hour or so while she went to town. Another asked for some home baking and a laundry service.

Situated directly opposite to the school was Chipchase House, and since the school opened the owner allowed staff to take children into the grounds to picnic and play in the long grass. When this house came on the market in 1960 Dr Ellis proposed the purchase of it. His long-term realistic vision was one of expansion of services for adults. The Chairman of the Executive Committee, Mr Frank Wilkin, was firmly opposed to such an idea. In 1964 Mr Hodgson, workshop manager, approached the Reyrolle management with the object of securing selected sub-assembly work for the centre on a sub-contracting basis. This was agreed to and Sid Richardson of the Production Engineering section was given the responsibility of organising the type and flow of work, which varied from small rotary switch contacts to solder-filled terminals. One of the most useful jobs was the assembly of studs, nuts and washers which were sent out to customers with each relay.

Chipchase House.

An occasion was arranged for these adult workers to visit the factory to see the results of their work.

In 1960 the first purpose built workshop was built in the grounds of Chipchase House. The house provided accommodation for thirty people while the workshop was extended to accommodate fifty-five day workers. The accommodation provided for residents was in dormitories for the majority. A condition for residency was daily attendance in the workshop. The first appointed manager of Chipchase House was Mr Tom Henderson with his wife Chris as the deputy, both of whom retired in 1993.

The Workshop at Chipchase House.

One morning in 1961 while covering my usual route to work I became aware that the contours of buildings ahead had altered overnight. The Embassy Ballroom situated on Station Road beside the gates of Chipchase House had burnt down. For the shop keepers situated below this spelt disaster. They stood aghast staring at smouldering embers. For many local residents it was a blessing and by 1966 for the Percy Hedley Centre it proved a bonus. The existing workshop was becoming over-crowded so the Trustees purchased the site and eventually a new Day Work Centre was opened on 19th June 1974 by Sir James Steel, CBE JP – the first Lord Lieutenant of the newly created county of Tyne & Wear. The Parents' Association under the direction of Stephen Darke played an active role in fundraising for this major development and the conversion of the old workshop into dining facilities.

Station Road, Forest Hall, in early 20th century.

During the construction of this building members of staff were invited by Gordon Crowther, the Administrator, to write messages in sealed envelopes which were incorporated within the cavity walls. That was a fun thing to do; some strange things lie within that brickwork.

Demand for residential accommodation gathered momentum and by 1985 an adjacent block of flats was built and the number of residents rose to forty.

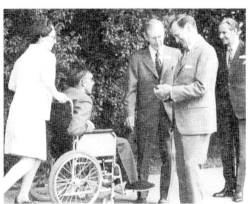

Sir James Steel (2nd right) at the officially opening of the new Day Work Centre.

When Ferndene House, adjacent to Chipchase, became vacant it was purchased by the Spastics' Society and remained unused for twenty-odd years. From time to time we, the staff, put forward a variety of ideas for demolition and development of the land. None proved acceptable or funding was unavailable at the time. Observing the development and present day provision on that site today, the wait for the opening of Ferndene Bungalows and the surrounding landscape in 1999 has proved well worthwhile.

The provision of therapy for adults was limited by time, by staffing ratios and appropriate facilities within the adult centre. Dorothy Thorpe was the first physiotherapist to go from the school on two mornings each week to work with adults. I followed her in the mid-sixties. Our role was ill-defined, our aims and objectives lacked precision. Dr Ellis was a paediatrician who accepted the role as consultant for adults until Dr Mike Barnes was appointed

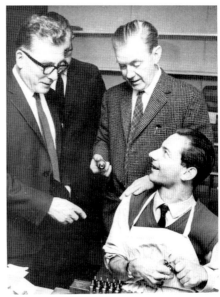

Mr E Ferrybrough, Department of employment, during his visit to the work centre with Mr J.A Hodgson, manager & Melvyn Ritchie.

Visiting Consultant in Rehabilitation in 1986. Our overall aim was to maintain mobility and function for each individual at the level already achieved. Also, to address specific problems whenever they arose. Against this background one had the freedom to carve out a role which would give a fair degree of professional service and job satisfaction. Conditions were not easy because support staff came from different backgrounds. There were no recognised training courses and little understanding of cerebral palsy or therapeutic interventions but above all about the importance of practice and generalisation of skills already learnt. After years of therapy sessions in school there were those who had had enough and lost the momentum to keep going. Others have remained well motivated and now in their late fifties and sixties retain a good level of mobility. The physiotherapist cannot operate in isolation and once Tom Henderson was appointed as Head of Adult Residential Care with his wife Chris as assistant living on the premises it was possible to gain greater co-operation. Together we constructed an in-service training programme which included lectures, circulation of papers and

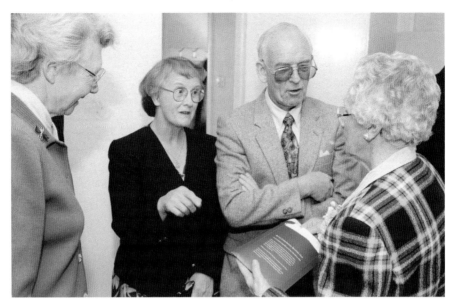

Mrs Alysoun Ellis, Chris & Tom Henderson & Mrs Molly Darke.

demonstrations. I was always of the opinion that all staff working with adults should learn and observe the work with small children. Likewise, staff in school should observe the outcome of their work with adults. This plan went some way towards motivating staff to play a more active rehabilitative role. An Occupational or Speech Therapist was not involved in the sixties and I adopted some aspects of their roles.

The first Occupational Therapist was employed in the school in 1971 and had made a valuable contribution but it was not until 1989 that Pauline Edwards was appointed to work with adults.

In 1983 Stewart Evans was appointed who held the post for three years before becoming the Head Occupational Therapist in 1986. Understandably, at that time, the adults did not have high expectations of further motor progress. After years of treatment the majority had little interest in physiotherapy and maintaining the degree of mobility which had been reached. As a result it proved difficult to motivate them and inactivity led on to weight increase in some cases. The appointment of an Occupational Therapist working permanently in the work shop broke the mould by introducing new ideas, new activities and focusing on tasks of daily living. This reinforced the aims and objectives of the physiotherapist and allowed me to turn my attention to group work.

Neil Murray and Ronnie Crozier making wire coathangers.

There were aspects of Conductive Education which I felt could be put into practice with a group of adults if only I could persuade them to co-operate. Also I needed assistance; Mrs Henderson proved to be enthusiastic and so it was that we were able to work with a group of ten all of whom were non ambulant and spent a great part of the day sitting in wheelchairs. Our first aim was to have everyone sitting freely on wooden boxes, unsupported. In the early stages all were fearful so our starting position was with the boxes against a wall. The next problem we encountered was their inability to bend down to pick an object off the floor without falling off the box. After regular sessions over three months all could sit freely and pick things up from the floor. We were accompanied by the music of Jimmy Shand, and I would claim that it was the psychological advantage of 'the group' the replacement of 'treatment' with education which proved to be the motivating factor.

A gift of a Solar Dome had been erected on the lawn for residents to sit in there on cool evenings. No-one ever sat there; weeds sprung up from the base and it became a white elephant. With full agreement from Tom I was allowed to pursue a gardening experiment with a small group including David Briggs (deceased), Tommy Leighton and David Moore and use the dome as a greenhouse. This was an evening activity and I had expected to remain closely involved. However, the project took off, the group became self supporting, productive and active. Each member contributed financially and David acted as the controller. Tommy was in receipt of the Royal Horticultural magazine. More knowledge was acquired and disseminated. More ambulant cerebral palsied friends joined the group to give their practical support and so it was that I became redundant in that area.

Gardening in the dome was limited and we needed to construct some raised beds. The derelict Ferndene site was just the place. Quite by chance Lewis Brown, Manager of Newman's Delicatessen, Newcastle, at the time asked Tom if he could do some voluntary work. After a consultation with me Lewis joined the gardeners and gave consistent help every week until he moved to Cumbria. With his help we had our raised beds. The next challenge was the acquisition of a purpose built greenhouse now that this group had demonstrated capability and genuine interest.

Over many years a group known as the Ponteland Spastics Group raised money for specific projects. One example still in existence is the Ponteland Way – the pathway which runs parallel to Station Road on the school side of the hedge. Each year David Johnson would ask Heads of Department for their suggestions on how to spend the money. The list would be sent to the fundraisers and they made the choice. I put forward a greenhouse for adults. Until that time a request for an adult facility had never been presented neither had it been expected. The school had always benefited, so we were delighted when the Ponteland Spastics Group selected the greenhouse.

Once this was erected the Ponteland Ladies were invited for an official opening ceremony at which the Chairman presented the gardeners with a grape vine.

David Briggs receiving a new greenhouse from the Chairman of Ponteland Ladies Group in 1978.

A chance encounter with Rob Moffatt, a writer, resulted in another group activity for students. Rob agreed to give his services voluntarily and during his time with the group they wrote a play – "It Just Takes a Second" which was based on the unfortunate experience of Peter Swanson. Peter had suffered serious head injuries when, on his way to a dinner dance, he was knocked down by a bus. Until his death in 2001, Peter remained a Chipchase resident. This play was suitable for production but funding could not be raised at the time to put it on stage.

It did occur to me that there were those in the workshop with good manual dexterity whereby they could be taught fly-tying. With this in mind I stepped into Newcastle tackle shop – Bagnall and Kirkwood in Grey Street. I asked if there was anyone they could recommend who would be willing to teach this skill to a small disabled group. This assistant had just returned to work part-time following his recovery from a stroke. With spare time on his hands he presented himself as a tutor the following week and for many months gave his services voluntarily. The interest led on to an encounter with Graham Simpson, a keen match angler who managed the Northern Bait Farm, Wylam. He arranged a competition there for disabled anglers on a small lake. He equipped all the competitors with rods, waterproof clothing and organised helpers who lived locally. The interest of the Percy Hedley Fishing Group led on to further expeditions and contact with Jack Charlton, a very keen angler. Graham Simpson organised and funded a trip to Bantry West Lodge Hotel in Eire for six fishermen plus helpers and their wives. Here, they joined up with an Irish contingent. The Irish made a return visit to Keilder Water to the competition organised by Jack Charlton, who set up the Jack Charlton Disabled Anglers' Trust.

Help for tying on the hook and bait was needed but hooking, controlling and landing a fish was within the range of all who joined this group. In 2010 some of those early anglers are still fishing.

Melvyn Ritchie receiving the Jack Charlton Disabled Anglers Trophy.

Cooking, Cleaning, Typing, Mending

Behind all the activity and behind all those who are the prime movers there lies an extensive array of people who are employed to keep the entire machine energised and on the road. Without reliable administrative support, domestic management, cleaners and technicians of quality the Percy Hedley Foundation would have ground to a halt. Some come and go, others will never be forgotten – Tom and Ernie slipped off our tongues like jam and bread.

Domestic, Secretarial and Support Staff, 1989. Back Row: Joan Dixon, Irene Hunter, Margaret Sherat, Anne Walker, Jackie Martin, Joan Vietch, Pam Welford, Joan Osborne, Kath Nugent, Doreen Dryden, Doreen Waggot. Middle row: Marie Tapson, Elsie McGahan, Edna Bryden, Mollie Stewart, Margaret McElderry, Pat Leetham, Joan Frazer. Front Row: Michelle Dunn, Betty Hopkins, Jackie Watson, Ernie Stone, Richard Baron, Alice Fee, Jackie Bloomfield, Susan Barnes.

Tom Irwin

Tom had been in post one year before me and his title was just 'Tom' because he made himself available for whatever job he was requested to do. Tom was an Irishman who had served in the RAF and had been posted to Singapore for two years. Following demobilisation he worked in the Formica factory on the Coast Road between 1956 and 1958 before he joined the Percy Hedley staff.

Tom was small, dapper with a neat moustache. He was always smart and along with his co-partner, Fred Lapsley, always wore uniform; lightweight beige jackets.

Fred was responsible for driving, vehicle maintenance and general duties. He had his base in the shed adjoining the main car park alongside the rubbish bins. He had a small desk, some drawers and boxes. Anyone requiring light bulbs, cleaning materials, soap and the like had to adhere to his strict rules regarding requests for such items. There were fixed times for staff to enter Fred's shed and everything and everybody was recorded in his ledger.

While Fred spent time in the shed or on the road Tom had his own private corner down under, in the boiler house. He could enter from outside behind the clinic building or through a small door leading from the main hall of Hampeth Lodge. A steep wooden staircase led down into the bowels of the building; a warm dusty Hobbit hole. Shelves held piles of records and other archival material.

Moving on, the next compartment was Tom's resting place and where he concocted but did not conceal or consume his home-brewed beer. Beyond this point was a large area housing wheelchairs, walking aids spare parts, obsolete equipment, sticks, wheels and a variety of footplates. A mighty mound of metal out of which came Tom's solution to an on-going avalanche of requests for spare parts, year upon year. When he was above ground he was on the run and this had a distinct psychological advantage. People are disinclined to waylay you and pile on another job if you are in a hurry. If they do all you need further in your armory is a fast flowing strong Irish accent delivered on the hoof and a footplate in your hand to act as a further deterrent.

To unearth Tom from his den meant shouting down wooden steps or going round the back. Or entering the brush cupboard located directly above 'the brewery'. In there was a loose knot in a plank through which you could shout and then replace the knot, which is what I did frequently. Tom took his responsibilities very seriously. Fixed tasks included weighing all children regularly and recording. Maintaining all the second hand tricycles which were donated and matching one to each child. Those requiring adaptations brought forth some ingenious notions. Tom enlisted the help of Mrs Hope-Poole, a member of the Management Committee, whose husband had unusually large feet to supply him with his cast off shoes. These he screwed to pedals and a child could then readily slide in a booted foot giving him the facility to hold the position. Lying under the plinth in the plaster room was a long, deep-red box – the coffin. From his main basement supply Tom kept this well stocked up with spare parts for our immediate use. Make do and mend was the order of the day.

His pool maintenance skills proved scientifically sound. There was daily testing of the water, servicing of the pump and filters. No-one knew his formula but no one ever changed colour or came out with blisters.

Tom Irwin with Susan Barnes on his retirement day.

Early morning rising for resident boys brought Tom into daily contact with children and care staff. Well after his retirement to the end of his life many past pupils kept in regular contact with him. He was a real gem of a fellow. Ernie Stone was appointed in 1977 as the technician and together they made a fine team.

Ernie Stone.

Ernie Stone

Ernie was born in Bedfordshire the son of a regular RAF serviceman. He eventually moved North and was educated at Ivy Road School, Forest Hall. He completed his National Service in the RAF before becoming an apprentice electrician. Once he became self-employed he was serving residents in the area which included the school, but mainly the adult centre. One of his first jobs was the removal of a lamp post from the middle of the school court yard and replacing it with a lamp on the wall. Ernie became attracted to the place so one day he was tipped off by a Chipchase employee, Ian Howson, that there was a need for a technician based in the school. Ernie went to see David Johnston and presented himself for the job. His first question was "Are you a family man?" His technical skills had been in evidence for some time; added to this he had a wife and three children. His communication skills, his sense of humour, good nature and relationship with children were the key to his success. He was available to all to solve technical problems and as such came up with some ingenious solutions: plastic keyboard covers for typewriters, expanding tables and adjustable arms for chairs were just a few.

Ernie was something of a wine maker so it was not unusual for him to join Tom in his break periods in the cellar. On one occasion David Johnston was looking for help and came upon the pair decanting Ernie's wine. "No problem" he said "it looks good so just come up when you're finished!" On another, Ernie came upon Tom trapped in the middle of his mettle mound with legs in the air and an arm through some spokes and had to be rescued. In and out of school they were good friends. Both loved the Christmas festivities, preparing for the entertainment, using reflector lights which Ernie had saved from disused clubs, decorating the tree and playing parts in the staff pantomime.

Eventually Ernie became a driver and accompanied staff and children on expeditions to the theatre, art galleries and places of interest. Time given to these activities was out of hours, voluntary work.

Tom and Ernie were a rare breed, we would have floundered without them.

Then came Ben. Ben Lyddon was described as driver/handyman and his day began at 7.30 am when he took all electric wheelchairs from the charging bay and distributed them to their owners when they arrived.

Next came a visit to the pool to test the waters for their chlorous and PH levels followed by routine maintenance of three ambulances. By 9.15 am Ben was outdoors in all weathers, supervising and directing traffic. This was no mean feat with limited available parking space for an ever increasing number of staff, children, visitors and car owners. In this situation Ben was in full command and needed to be to avoid chaos at the end of the day. Between these two daily hectic events he was busy with on-going repairs and adaptations but always at the ready for a wide range of requests; children to be taken for hospital appointments, equipment to be collected or parcels to go to the post office. For Ben this was all in the day's work.

Ben Lyddon.

For all who have ever passed along corridors, moved into classrooms and bedrooms they have always been clinically clean and attractive. To maintain such standards in a difficult building requires a willing workforce amenable to sound management and to be appreciated.

Our food was tastefully prepared, the menus varied and always ready on time. Christmas dinner was a great occasion and in the early years turkeys were cooked in the kitchen. Once all were assembled the hatch was lifted and behind stood Dr Ellis in chef's hat and apron ready to carve. As the

Retirement Day 1991 for Susan Frater. Edith Briggs (Domestic Bursar) Rosemary Pattison, Elsie Ferguson and Margaret Ashford – all cakes courtesy of Mrs Briggs.

number of pupils rose it was not possible to continue this homely practice. However, Christmas dinner has always remained a joyous occasion in the school and always one child has expressed appreciation for the great work done by staff in the kitchen throughout the year.

By 1992 Alice Fee had to ensure provision of interesting, balanced meals for two hundred and twenty-two people every day. Calculating amounts to avoid waste and ensuring food is of good quality is no mean task. Within one month, 150 loaves of bread, 220 packets of cornflakes and 2464 lbs of potatoes were consumed. Variety is important and menus were planned for a month and not immediately repeated. Account had to be taken of particular needs of those children with feeding or weight problems who required an attractive appetising solution. As school provided many extra curricular activities, educational visits and day trips it called for additional preparation in the kitchen, often at short notice.

To cook and clean in the kitchen in 1992 there was a staff of twelve working two shifts 8 am – 3 pm and 4.15 pm – 7.45 pm. Domestic staff were on duty 7.30 am – 9 am and 3 pm – 7 pm All were involved with the children in different ways. Resident children would tell their news or help those cleaning in the evenings. Domestic staff accompanied children and teachers on their outings and helped with clubs. They made a valuable contribution and delighted in the children's progress.

They never let the pans burn dry. Dr Ellis always claimed that visitors to the school would not complain about any aspect if they were well served – given a good lunch. They never did and oh how they envied us having those home-made shortbread biscuits at coffee time!

Above: Percy Hedley School catering Staff in 1988.

Right: Betty Hopkins and Jackie Bloomfield, Administration Staff, at a sports day.

Money Matters

Although the teaching, therapy and care staff were not responsible for raising or management of funds we were conscious of the need for frugality and we were made aware of periods of financial crises. If at any time demands appeared extravagant David Johnston would recount "The Pensioner's Tale".

Every few months running over a few years an old man and his dog would present themselves at the reception desk and deliver £50 of savings. He was a widower, who had walked from Wallsend to Forest Hall and he was always invited to have a cup of tea and a chat with David Johnston and that was it. He was a generous, modest man with no desire for further attention or involvement. "Always keep that in mind", said David Johnston. "That £50 was hard earned. An old man has consistently walked the distance to hand it over. We must spend it wisely".

Money matters and every little counts. The Friends of the Spastic Children North East Area became a registered charity.

Joe Harvey, captain of Newcastle United and Mrs Molly Darke auctioning a cake replica of the FA Cup – won three times by Newcastle in the 1950s.

The committee was formed to co-ordinate efforts in areas of publicity, fundraising and accepting responsibility for the foundation of a centre.

In July 1952 the 'Scrap Metal Drive' was launched and on Friday, 12th September The Lord Mayor of Newcastle, Mrs V H Graham, presented a cheque for £770. The Oriana Choir Gateshead held a celebrity concert. The proceeds were directed to aid the funds. The Lord Mayor nominated the charity to receive profits from the Gosforth Central Players' production of 'Young Wives' Tale' on 18th November 1952. These are just a few examples of efforts made in the early years along with the increasing publicity they attracted.

From hereon a Management Committee and a Medical Advisory Committee were created. Whilst it became apparent that the former were gradually taking responsibility for some key fundraising events and the original mission of Friends of the Spastic Children North East Area had been accomplished it was decided that they should cease to function.

The registration of the original charity was then transferred to the Percy Hedley School Management Committee.

On 31st January 1956 the Parents' Association was created but it was not be regarded as a sub-committee of the Percy Hedley School Management Committee. It was seen as a separate body which would have close association with the latter. The aim of this association was to give on-going individual support to the Percy Hedley Centre. Two of the founder members were on the Management Committee.

In 1955 the Parents' Association bought a Bedford Dormobile. Over the years their efforts resulted in financial contributions towards the major projects in particular providing facilities for adults.

Mr Stephen Darke was the Honorary Secretary and Treasurer. He was very active in organising holidays for parents and in 1973 he acquired two caravans for hire at the Whitley Bay Lighthouse Caravan Park. In the same year two draws were held over Christmas and Race Week.

Between 1953 and 1965 financial management and administration were the responsibility of Mr Harry Severs who was succeeded by Mr Gordon Crowther. Between 1965 and 1989 Gordon Crowther steered the centre through times of financial stringency as well as being party to many rewarding events. Over and above his professional standing for this difficult role he had particular social advantages. He was a

Gordon and Monica Crowther with Chris Johnston.

good communicator with a consistent temperament. Because he enjoyed group activities and social occasions he was a 'people person' ideally suited for all manner of fundraising events, cultivating good relationships and generating publicity. Members of staff were often persuaded to accompany him on occasions when a donation was being made and so it was in this context that I paid my first visits to a dog stadium, a motor cycle racing track and danced the night away in the Lyons Club.

Tucked away in his own corner and supported by a small team of administrators he was able to ride out some stormy periods when finances were strained and the unexpected came to the surface. For example, cash reserves had built up but were eroded between 1968 and 1972 firstly by the building of the school extensions. Secondly, by building the new work centre followed by alterations in Chipchase House which altogether totalled £200,000.

Every year the Fire Brigade and the Health & Safety Executive visited and their suggestions were always addressed. In 1979 one which caused concern was to make all bedroom doors in Chipchase House 'half-hour fire resistant, hinged and self-closing' which proved very costly when coupled with costs for additional maintenance features on three lifts. Running costs for the centre were rising and winter weather brought snow and severe frost that year causing gallons of water to pour through the felt roof of the workshop which had to be repaired at a cost of £5,000.

In 1969 The Million Shilling Appeal was launched to raise £50,000 for the building of the new work centre and so solve the problem of overcrowding. A public relations company was employed to organise the fund. The Lord Mayor of Newcastle, WRS Forsyth, Bob Monkhouse, wealthy individuals, companies, schools and colleges were approached in an attempt to raise the Million Shillings. Members of the Parents' Association under their Secretary, Mr S F Darke, were very active in organising a flag day, holding public collections at the Tyneside Agricultural Show and at Newcastle Races during Race Week.

The final result proved disappointing in spite of wide media publicity and advertising. The net amount raised from the Appeal was £6,394.

Singer Eve Boswel helping Fundraising for
The Million Shilling Appeal.

Coldgate Mill

A most exciting thing occurred when Mr William Alexander Smith bequeathed his property, Coldgate Mill, to the centre in 1982. Coldgate Mill lies just south of Wooler at North Middleton, Northumberland. It consisted of a large workshop with a flat above. Linked to it was the house which had a lounge, bedroom, kitchen and bathroom and toilet on the ground floor. Upstairs were two further bedrooms. All members of staff were most enthusiastic about using this as their very own field study centre. It offered opportunities for outdoor education and independence training and was in an area of natural beauty.

William A. Smith

It required furnishing and decorating and funds had to be raised to do it. The Headmistress, the Ponteland Ladies' Association and the Parents' Association worked hard to achieve the necessary amount required. By 1983 the mill had been used for one full week and several weekends by various groups of children accompanied by staff. Unfortunately a number of factors combined to make the mill an unviable project. After visits over three seasons it was not being used often enough to merit the maintenance costs. Furthermore, following a fire inspection report, if the recommendations had been implemented it would have changed the character of the mill. In 1986 a decision was taken to sell (following a long and complicated transaction) and the Percy Hedley Centre benefited by over £50,000 from the sale. The money was placed in a separate fund which was used for children's holidays in another form.

HMS Newcastle

In the early eighties the Percy Hedley School was chosen by HMS *Newcastle*, a Royal Navy Type 42 Destroyer to be its sponsor school. Over the years the ship's complement of two hundred and eighty men have been kept informed of pupils' progress and all developments. There have been many visits from crew members and their efforts to provide computers, technical units and items of equipment have been appreciated. The School/Navy Liaison Officer reported annually on these exciting visits and donations and kept the children well informed throughout the year on the ship's movements, position and activities.

Staff and children visit HMS Newcastle.

This ship was the eighth to carry the name and was launched at the Swan Hunter shipyard on the Tyne in April 1975 and was involved in operations in the Atlantic and Mediterranean oceans. In 2004 HMS *Newcastle* was decommissioned.

Without the continuous flow of generous donations, legacies and covenanted subscriptions our progress would have been sorely impaired, our enterprises unrealised, the children and adults deprived. It could be claimed that the Percy Hedley Foundation is a symbol of North East generosity spread over sixty-five years.

Three Crew members with Greg Draper, John Appleby and David Purvis.

As the foundation continued to grow in response to need, it became clear that new and expanded accommodation was required if the charity was to continue to meet this need and provide the highest quality of service.

Central to this was the launch of a major fundraising appeal in 1996 and the recruitment of prominent Appeal Patrons and an influential Fundraising Appeal Committee. The first head Appeal Patron was Sir Ralph Carr-Ellison, Lord Lieutenant of Tyne & Wear, who recruited John Ward and George Ross as the joint chairs of what became an extremely active Appeal Committee. Over the next ten years approximately £10 million was raised to redevelop the Day Centre, build bungalows on the Chipchase site, create a new Percy Hedley senior school and Post-16 Centre and Sports Academy, as well as other specialist projects.

Dr R L Townsin (Chairman of the Board of Trustees), Jim Ferris, Sir Ralph and Lady Carr-Ellison, Keith Lorraine (Enterprise 5 Housing Association) with resident Peter Swanson celebrating the opening of Ferndene Housing in 1999.

50th Anniversary – A New School

In 2003, 50 years after her mother The Duchess of Kent opened the original Percy Hedley School, HRH Princess Alexandra officially opened the new Percy Hedley Senior School on the Bradbury Campus in Killingworth. She met with students involved in a project highlighting the school's 50 year history and was presented with an album of photographs from her mother's visit by Percy Hedley residents who were pupils during her mother's visit. She also met with Mr and Mrs Stephen Darke, the parents who led the campaign over 50 years before.

Those Special Occasions

There were so many days in the school calendar, year after year, which brought both pleasure and publicity: fun days, picnics, trips to the theatre and sporting events. Visits from VIPs – stage and sporting personalities, civic dignitaries and royalty.

The first special occasion was the visit of Her Royal Highness, the Duchess of Kent on 16th February 1954 exactly one year after the school opened. This gave the staff great encouragement because she understood the nature of cerebral palsy and appreciated the efforts that had been made to establish the school.

1969 was the year when Hilda Shield, Deputy Headteacher, was made a Member of the Order of the British Empire in the New Year's Honours List. In the same year Dr Ellis visited the United States to observe the development of treatment centres for cerebral palsy. Headteacher David Johnston received sponsorship by the Winston Churchill Travelling Fellowship to visit the United States to study educational aspects and participate in a summer course.

This indeed was recognition of their fine achievements and contributed to the renown of the school. Added to this the school children were successful in events at the Spastic Games at Stoke Mandeville and made their particular contribution to keeping the Percy Hedley Centre at the forefront of organisations catering for those with cerebral palsy.

Many local, national and international sporting events have been recorded when Percy Hedley School pupils have been successful in both individual and team events.

Mr Frank Wilkin greeting HRH The Duchess of Kent at the official opening of Percy Hedley School.

In 1965 Mr Alan Brown, lecturer in Physical Education at the University of Newcastle and father of a child with cerebral palsy, started a project to explore ways in which sports and games could be adapted so that even the most disabled children could take part. The project had appeal and many sports firms and other companies contributed to the purchase or adaptation of equipment. Alan Brown worked closely with Pauline Adair, the physiotherapist responsible for group work in the gym whereby appropriate programmes and progressions were created. His contribution to the interest and development of sporting activities cannot be over-estimated. In athletics 11 boys and 1 girl were highly successful in the Second National Spastic Games at Stoke Mandeville where they accumulated a total of thirty-two Gold, twenty Silver and seven Bronze medals.

On 22nd and 23rd July 1974, fourteen past and present pupils took part in the First International Games held at the National Sports Centre, Crystal Palace. The Percy Hedley pupils made up 20% of the Great Britain team and fourteen other countries were involved. On 16th June 1982 at the University of Newcastle Sports Ground, Cochrane Park, one hundred and fifty-seven competitors from nineteen schools and centres took part in the twelfth Northern Counties Games. They came from Cleveland, Cumbria, Lancashire and North Yorkshire. These games were run on rules laid down by the International Sports and Recreation Association of the Cerebral Palsy Society.

Success in this field continued and their abilities in sport have taken many to events in Portugal, France, West Germany, Denmark, Norway and the USA.

Stephen Miller started school in 1983, aged three years, and in spite of his severe motor handicap made such progress that he was able, at the age of ten, to transfer into mainstream education. However, being very keen on sport he continued to attend Percy Hedley Sports Club and always had the ambition to win a Gold medal in the Olympic Games one day. Stephen has been successful in three successive Olympic Games winning gold medals for Club Throwing. In 2008 he entered his fourth Olympics. In May 2005 he was invited to lay the Foundation Stone for the new Academy for Disability Sports, officially opened by Her Royal Highness, The Princess Royal on 11th October 2005.

Above: Stephen Miller, aged 5 years.

Right: Stephen with his Gold Medals.

On the afternoon of 9th December 1982 Kevin Keegan, of Newcastle United Football Club, visited the school and the residents in Chipchase House. There he delighted them with yarns about his experiences in an amusing and informative manner.

Kevin Keegan returned to Percy Hedley when he became manager of Newcastle United.

In 1989 ex-England footballer, Sir Trevor Brooking, spent a day touring the school and gave some team coaching. This was part of a prize won by Steven Wood whilst he had been successful in winning a penalty prize competition at Wembley Stadium as part of the Football League celebrations.

On Wednesday, 19th June 1974 the new Day Work Centre was opened by Sir James Steel, CBE JP fourteen years after the opening of the first workroom on the old RAF station, Whitley Road, Benton where sixteen workers had attended daily.

In September 1991 the Lynx helicopter crew of HMS *Newcastle* performed a skilful manoeuvre over Chipchase House and brought down the craft onto the lawn much to the delight of children. They were then given an opportunity to sit inside the helicopter and talk to the crew.

Christmas was always exciting and joyful for the children and staff put in a great deal of time and effort to make it memorable. Between half term and Christmas each class practised their pantomime which was performed during the week before Christmas lunch and the annual visit of Santa Clause. Christmas 1971 and we had the pleasure of Jimmy Logan, a great Scottish entertainer who died in 2001. Jimmy Logan was a household name as an actor, musician, comedian and he certainly entertained us all on that occasion.

Jimmy Logan and David Johnston dancing with children at a Christmas party in 1971.

25th June 1983 was a proud day of 30th Anniversary celebrations when ninety-five old boys and girls attended for a reunion. They came from many parts of the country and some were accompanied by husbands or wives. They were welcomed by staff, past and present and all delighted in renewing old friendships. The sun shone all day and the kitchen staff prepared beautiful table decorations and excellent food. On the walls were pictures covering the previous thirty years added to which many had brought their own photograph albums. There were two more celebratory parties, one for the present pupils and another for staff which was also a retirement party for Mrs Sadie McKensie who was an original staff member appointed as a classroom assistant in the infants' class.

Elaine Boyd, from Warkworth, Northumberland, was a lively minded resident child who made good contact with celebrities. Stephen Hendry, the snooker player, was one who had given her encouragement. When she learnt that Princess Diana was visiting the region in 1989 Elaine sent a request inviting her to visit the school. This was accepted and confirmed after a team from the Palace made a visit to inspect the building, the facilities and security. There were consultations with police and civic personnel before the plan was finalised.

On 12th July 1989, a glorious warm summer's day, the physiotherapy room was commandeered by police security guards and sniffer dogs. Tom and Ernie were on duty in the court yard, which had been scoured the previous day by Local Authority employees to remove all oil and petrol marks. Now they were awaiting the arrival of Local Authority vehicles carrying an array of floral displays. This was the biggest clean-up ever. Come early afternoon we all had our designated positions. Parents of the youngest children were with them in the court yard and Elaine was in a prime position alongside the welcoming party; the Chairman, Mr Neil Murray, his wife, members of the Management Committee and the Headteacher, Jim Ferris. The selected route passed along 'the Ponteland Way' which runs parallel to the hedge and in 1989 the outstretched arms of many local residents crossed over it to greet the princess. Today it would be too high.

The traffic was halted, the police were in position and all went quiet at the sound of motor bike outriders roaring down Station Road, Forest Hall and swinging in through the main gates. Children had flowers to present and their excitement

mounted as Princess Diana approached. I was standing behind
Craig Raine, aged 9 years, clutching his bouquet. She stood
before him and with arms extended he pronounced "These are
for you, your Majesty". Her response, her spontaneous
reactions and warmth will remain for ever in the memories of
those who were there.

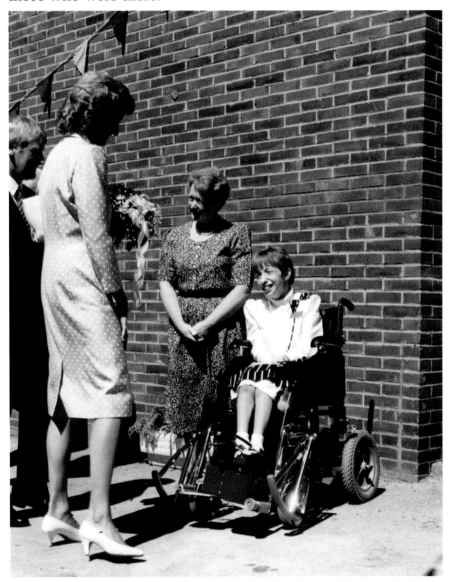

*Princess Diana meeting Elaine Boyd who invited her to visit the
school.*

Ronnie meets Princess Diana with Sylvia Patterson, domestic science teacher, looking on.

Princess Diana with children in the classroom.

Princess Diana meeting children and parents.

Leila Scott, Infant's teacher meeting Princess Diana.

The Start of Something New

Following retirement in July 1992 I could reflect on what had been an exciting and rewarding working life. I left with memories of many parents who demonstrated resilience and worked steadfastly with their children and gave them a life. Memories of children who had strived and overcame many obstacles. There were no miracles only success stores. It was against this background that we, the staff, shared our thoughts and opinions, exposed our strengths and weaknesses, found some lasting friendships and in so doing were able to perpetuate an ethos which has resulted in continuous progress.

Without a well-defined retirement plan I found myself attracted towards some unexpected opportunities. Over the years many contacts had been made in the UK and abroad through the Conductive Education Association, through Scope and in particular through previous visits to Poland and Hungary. Added to this was the reputation of the Percy Hedley Foundation which was my passport.

In 1993 I received a request from Maureen Lilley, the Director of the Hornsey Centre for Conductive Education, London to be become involved in staff training. This centre was the brain child of Ester Cotton and Dr Lillemor Jernquist and had been running for three years. Both had been responsible for staff training. Ester wished to retire and Lillemor had accepted the new role of first Director of the Craighalbert Centre, Cumbernauld, Scotland. I accepted the invitation and for the next seven years spent one week each month in London. The Hornsey Centre ran a number of courses which I helped to design and to which I contributed. In particular were the day courses for teachers in mainstream schools who were encountering more children with special needs as the inclusion policy was being implemented. Our day course entitled "A Child with Cerebral Palsy in the Classroom" was always well subscribed.

Between times the contact with Poland was maintained and started to expand. As more and more requests for help were arriving I needed to seek financial support which came eventually from a charitable organisation, British Executive Service Overseas (BESO) which has now amalgamated with VSO. This charity was established to attract retired business and professional people to share their skills in under-developed countries where there were BESO agents appointed

Agata Zych, physiotherapist, working with a group in Zagorze, Poland.

to manage the assignments. With this support and an escalating interest in Conductive Education in Poland the visits averaged three a year. As a result more centres were springing up, more courses were being arranged. After six years I had visited five centres in Warsaw, two in Krakow, one each in Wroclaw, and Zamosc (a small town in South East Poland not far from the Ukranian border). There were many return visits, particularly to Zamosc where I detected early on that here it would be possible to develop the Krok za Krokiem (Step by Step) centre as a model of conductive education practice for Poland.

As a result of these early interventions together with the dynamism and determination of the Director, Dr Maria Krol, finance was obtained through European funding for on-going visits and exchanges between staff from Zamosc and the Percy Hedley Foundation. Without co-operation this degree of development would not have been achieved in Poland.

It may well appear that these expeditions required time and hard work. It was all worthwhile, the rewards proved immeasurable and they cost me nothing in financial terms. I learnt enough of the language to speak directly with the children and to survive. Add to this list history, geography and

Dr Maria Krol and her staff with Percy Hedley Headmaster, Norman Stromsoy.

culture but above all living their life in their homes, forming new friendships and enjoying their generous hospitality.

I did question how it could be that on 15th December 2000 I was invited to attend a ceremony in the Polish Embassy to receive from the Polish Ambassador the Knights' Cross of the Order of Merit of the Republic of Poland. I made clear at the time that without on-going support from the Percy Hedley Foundation the dispersion of knowledge in Polish centres would not have happened.

Between times there were other adventures. In 1996 came an invitation from Geoff Smirthwaite to accompany him and his wife to the USA to attend the annual conference of occupational therapists to be held in Baltimore. Geoff (based in Newton Abbot) was the supplier of our special furniture. He had served us well and took a keen interest in the development of Conductive Education in the UK and was a CE Association member. Four thousand people attended over three days to view an exhibition of equipment and to attend lectures. In return for this opportunity I had to present a paper and show the Percy Hedley film "Learning for Living" which supported Geoff's sales pitch. Following this event we spent three days in Washington DC.

In 1998 I received a request from Anita Loring, the Secretary General of the International Cerebral Palsy Society, to present a paper at the first Middle East Cerebral Palsy Conference to be held in Beirut. A few attempts had been made previously to hold this event but they had to be aborted due to the potential fragility in the Lebanon following the long conflict with Israel. Finally it happened and in October 1998. I arrived at a very dilapidated Beirut airport and was checked and re-checked to ensure that at no time had I ever visited Israel. This initial journey took me through a continuum of battered, bullet ridden, war-torn buildings. A truly sad sight in a most beautiful country.

This four day conference had a different international flavour from those I had ever attended in the West. I had to measure with care quite different cultural attitudes. This initial contact led on to four more visits over the next six years to run courses, to advise and to enjoy Lebanese hospitality together with my colleagues, Anita Loring and Carol Hughes who was headteacher at White Lodge School between 1972 – 1985. Anita co-ordinated all aspects of our programme and acted as the scribe leaving teacher and therapist to demonstrate practical help.

Through working side by side with the staff teams and families of the Lebanese centres we were able to identify areas of weakness in professional practice. Our response to this was to offer workshops on subjects as varied as: the importance of purpose built equipment, inter-disciplinary practice, team meetings, record keeping and teaching the profoundly disabled child with severe learning difficulties. Over the course of one trip we assessed in excess of fifty children with their families.

On one occasion we experienced, briefly, life inside a Palastinian refugee camp. In spite of the unacceptable cramped living conditions, behind some corrugated metal sheets, there was a small acceptable centre for cerebral palsied children who attended daily. On return home, with co-operation of Headteacher, Norman Stromsoy, and Percy

Teaching and Learning in a Palastinian Refugee Camp.

Hedley staff it was possible to arrange two visits which proved very helpful for the Lebanese. First for the Director and Head Physiotherapist from Sesobel Centre, Beirut and at a later date and a longer period, three staff members for training.

My last visit to Lebanon was in 2004 only one month after the assassination of the popular President Rafal Harire. The Syrians had departed after many years as a peace keeping force but there remained the occasional bomb explosion occurring in the suburbs after 6.00 pm. Sadly my attempts to return to Lebanon have been thwarted by continuing political turbulence and the possibility of hostilities being resumed. Meantime, I am thankful for the messages I receive giving particular progress reports and news of the Sesobel Centre's survival.

This triple act was repeated in Athens in 2003. However, our greatest adventure took us to Nepal for two weeks in Spring 2004. This was at the invitation of Professor Rajbhandari who was Executive Director of the Self Help Group for Cerebral Palsy in Nepal. Professor Rajbhandari was a retired engineer and he had chosen to devote his years of retirement to establishing services for children with cerebral palsy. As well as a centre in Kathmandu he had set in motion an out-reach programme for many living in remote areas of the Himalayas. Small teams of health workers were operating in different areas under the guidance of a psychologist and a German physiotherapist, Sabine Dreeman.

Carol Hughes observing walking practice in a Nepalise Village.

Before responding to any request received by ICPS Anita Loring ensured that we had as much information as possible before agreeing to undertake an assignment. From thereon we would have a number of meetings to formulate our action plan and identify our individual responsibilities. For my part this involved visits to the Percy Hedley School to continually update knowledge, acquire copies of recent publications, borrow a pair of arm splints and a few video recordings.

On every foreign tour we had to adapt our basic programme and so became quite adept at thinking on our feet, responding appropriately to strange sets of circumstances, communicating and interacting between ourselves by way of expression and gesture. It was necessary to familiarise oneself with religious and cultural aspects before attempting to win over the minds of those we hoped to influence. This was particularly the case in Nepal.

Our Team in Kathmandu – Suzi Groeli (our guide), Olive Surtees, Anita Loring, Carol Hughes and Sabine Dreeman.

Once more we found ourselves in the midst of dangerous conflict. For some years there had been on-going hostility between the army under the direction of the King of Nepal and Maoist guerrillas. Attacks took place mainly in the villages but sporadic strikes took place in Kathmandu. Shops were forbidden to open or taxis to operate and without the latter in narrow streets workers could not reach the workplace unless on bike or foot. Anyone failing to comply risked a bomb or a shot. During our visit three such strikes were called and this might well have disrupted our programme if we had not come up with an alternative plan. We arranged with our hotel manager to take over the roof restaurant and continue our training there. The Director, Professor Rajbhandari, and fifteen staff came on foot or bikes and so we continued the work as well as entertaining our group under the sun and providing lunch.

At the weekend we joined Sabine Dreeman and were transported in a minibus on the main route to Tibet up into the Kathmandu valley to embark on some pre-arranged home visits. Although there was a risk of confrontation with bands of Maoists I was assured that they were not really interested in kidnapping "white haired old English women'. This was rough terrain and our bus could only go so far. The rest was foot work for two or three miles. On the steepest stretches I had one man pulling me upfront while another pushed from behind. When we reached the first hamlet composed of primitive dwellings the entire community, old and young, surrounded us in cross-legged sitting on the ground, together with goats and hens. They were waiting for a miracle. On one occasion we were presented with a lively four year old boy who had uncontrolled movements of arms and legs. He was eager to stand up and walk but very frustrated because he could not construct the right strategy. Glancing around I saw a stick heap and some bamboo poles. We asked for a hatchet to trim the bamboo and some rope to lash to the back of chairs which were standing outside. Now we had our parallel bars and with more hatchet work we had a variety of short sticks

The Nepalese villagers with a hatchet.

to be used to teach grasp and release. Our Nepalese assistants by now were well aware of the requirements and what needed to be explained and taught while we demonstrated. With gentle persuasion the little boy co-operated. This remote mountain community rejoiced and over time the outreach team continued the programme with progressions.

The physiotherapist, Sabine Dreeman, returned to Germany for a few months and during that time she stayed with me for two weeks. She was welcomed by the Percy Hedley staff and afforded daily opportunities to observe and learn more about the practice before returning to Nepal. We remain in contact and I receive regular progress reports. Within a year the four year old learnt to walk independently and was able to attend the local school. A girl, aged twelve, who had spent all her time sitting on the ground with her back to the wall surrounded by the hens and goats can now sit unsupported on a wooden box and feed herself. We started her programme on an upturned waste paper basket before explaining to her father what was required.

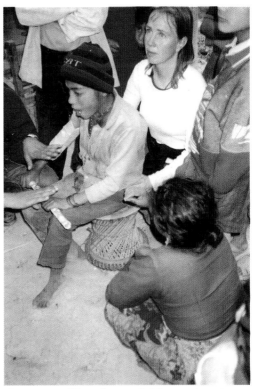

If I am fortunate enough to retain good health and the political situation remains calm in Nepal I might just get back there next year or accept another similar invitation which might come my way to keep the ageing brain alive. So thank you Percy Hedley for giving me, the children, their parents and the staff – A LIFE!

A young Nepalese girl learning to sit on an upended waste basket with Sabine Dreeman.

Conclusion

To institute a special school and clinic in the 1950s was not a task for the faint hearted. The process began with the recognition of a need by a small group of parents and supporters with a realistic, realizable vision. This was a group who had the tenacity to surmount all manner of obstacles, steer through turbulent times and survive. These were parents who simultaneously were going to work, managing a family and caring for a child with cerebral palsy.

The founding Trustees were manifestly wise in the manner in which they constructed their committees, sub-committees, business plan and lines of communication as well as the selection of unpaid members with particular areas of expertise. In their wisdom the Parent's Association of the Friends of the Spastic Children, North East Area, recognised the limitations of their role and eventually confined their activities to fundraising and practical support when requested. Their vision had been realized.

When, in 2003, the Percy Hedley Foundation celebrated fifty years of progress it was both moving and heartening because Stephen and Molly Darke were there to recount the tales of early endeavour: how they collected pennies in pubs and washed them in the bath before banking. They had survived and were able to witness the result of their efforts, and rejoice.

For me this style of development and management was brought into sharp focus when I began work in Poland. My remit was to introduce the philosophy and practical aspects of conductive education but it soon became apparent that no consideration had been given to the importance of sound management.

Molly and Stephen Darke.

50 years Anniversary Celebration. Back row: Molly Darke, Lily Longbottom, Olive Surtees, Rosemary Pattison, Hilda Shield, David Johnston, Dr. E. Ellis. Front row: Stephen L. Darke, Margaret Caines, Margaret McHugh, Stephen Darke and Jenny Young.

The infrastructure essential for good practice was either non-existent or ill-constructed. I could not convince the Directors, who were usually parents of cerebral palsied children, that my contribution as a physiotherapist would have limited effect unless this problem was addressed. However, it would be unimaginable that even the most basic training in this area would be accepted if delivered by me. This revelation resulted in the introduction of Norman Stromsoy and Lynn Watson, the head teachers to come to the rescue. I had never worked with either before but their willingness to co-operate epitomises the ethos of the Foundation and (as well as hard work) we did have some fun. This was the beginning of continuous co-operation between Polish centres and the Foundation which remains on-going. The importance of sound management, organisation, planning, communication, staff selection, mutual support, teamwork, goal setting and above all parent participation are the fundamental requisites for success in any area covered by any employee in any capacity where each and all are respected not only for their skills but for who they are, what they do and the contribution they make is revealed in this tale.

From Mollie Cauldwell, headteacher and Val Culloty, physiotherapist to Lynn Watson and Anne Coates holding those same posts today the aims and values have remained constant; to work harmoniously together, to learn from each other, to negotiate and solve problems. Without the fusion of therapy with education radical changes over fifty years could not have been made. Least of all with the introduction of Conductive Education.

This is but a brief history scanning 50 years, covering some key events seen through the eye of one who was there. It is claimed that you should not step back into the workplace, but I find this irresistible. Even though the number of recognisable faces is dwindling, the welcome at the reception desk remains constant. There is often a chat on a corridor with a passing child. The "coffin" lies no longer under the plinth in the plaster room but if you go in there on a Thursday morning, Eddie Weldon's big canvas bag of boots and splints will be resting above. I have never ventured down into the boiler house – Tom's Hobbit Hole – to inspect his mound of metal or to detect the smell of his last brew or called his name down a hole in the brush cupboard, but I do detect that there is something of him and all those key players long since gone, still lingering there. All have left a legacy.

Steven Lawrence, Neil and Tommy, live to this day in Chipchase House; comfortable attractive accommodation set in delightful grounds with freedom to make choices, meet friends and move around within the local community of Benton and Forest Hall. The community which once had such limited knowledge of cerebral palsy, was wary at first but grew to accept and understand the Percy Hedley children and adults and made them feel welcome and comfortable within their community; in the hair dressing salon, in shops, on the allotment with the pigeon fanciers, in Black's Newsagents and the Fusilier. In their way, like so many supporters, they have contributed to the success of this Foundation.

To Steven, Neil and Tommy today, I am just an old friend passing through and together we await the next chapter in a tale that I have been privileged to tell.

Stephen Lawrence Darke, Neil Murray and Tommy Leighton in 2011.

How people are treated in the workplace
is the main factor in their
job satisfaction, stress level and productivity.
Praise is important, work is about feeling valued.
"It is about a search for daily meaning
as well as daily bread,
for recognition as well as cash,
for astonishment rather than torpor.
In short for a sort of life rather than a
Monday through to Friday sort of dying"

Studs Terkel From his book 'Working' 1974

The Percy Hedley Foundation 2003 to 2011

Since the Foundation celebrated fifty years of progress in 2003 it has continued to grow and develop.

A purpose built, state of the art centre for Percy Hedley's post-16 students opened in 2004. The same year, discussions started between the Foundation and the Trustees of Northern Counties School for Deaf Children in Jesmond. It was agreed that a merger would benefit both organisations and this took place in October 2005. The Northern Counties' site now has a specialist nursery, college and a thriving school.

2005 also saw the launch of the Percy Hedley Academy for Disability Sports. The centre enables young people and adults to access sport regardless of their level of disability. This has been a major success and the facility has been accepted as a training facility for the 2012 Paralympics. In 2010 Tony Blair visited the Academy to launch a new partnership between Percy Hedley and the Tony Blair Sports Foundation. The Academy now trains disabled people as volunteer helpers and coaches, affording new opportunities to young disabled people in a sporting arena.

Joanne Hesler, from Foundation Radio, interviewing Tony Blair.

Beth Helliwell with artwork she created in iMuse.

2007 saw the launch of Linskill, a community base in North Shields for disabled adults. Our therapeutic approach introduces service users to a spa pool, sensory room, rebound therapy and iMuse – a pioneering facility that uses sensors triggered by movements as small as the blink of an eye. Even those service users with profound and complex needs can experience being in control of music and visuals at the Linskill centre.

In 2008 Jim Ferris, the Foundation's first Chief Executive retired after 23 years at the Foundation. He was awarded an OBE for his outstanding contribution to the well-being of disabled people. His position was taken over by Dr Tony Best. Services for adults have been developed with a unit on the Orion Business Park, in North Shields, where disabled people have the chance to try out a range of work skills. The site includes a purpose built catering unit which provides service users with experience in catering, a music department equipped with keyboard synthesisers, drum machines, sound samplers and sound beams, which help make music accessible to everyone. The multi-media department offers the full range of video production facilities and the latest addition is Foundation Radio, where regular podcasts are produced to showcase service users' work.

In 2009 the Foundation adopted a new 5-year plan that introduced an emphasis on research and evaluation of innovative services, and disseminating its knowledge through publications and a new website. In 2010 Her Royal Highness The Princess Royal was at the Foundation to officially open a new pioneering Centre for Conductive Education. Developed for adults with motor disorder disabilities, the centre has already transformed the lives of adults who have had a stroke, have Parkinson's or Multiple Sclerosis. The centre now delivers over 700 sessions per year and is supporting over 100 adults per month with acquired neurological disorders.

Her Royal Highness Princess Anne enjoying her visit.

So today, with over 550 staff and a turnover of more than £15m, the Percy Hedley Foundation is one of the largest regional charities. This size enables the Foundation to provide a wide range of services to more than 1000 families each year.

Today the Percy Hedley Foundation offers:

Children's Services

Percy Hedley Children's Services meet the needs of children with cerebral palsy, hearing or visual impairments and speech, language and communication difficulties. As a regional specialist provider the Foundation does not belong to any local education authority and admits children from anywhere in the country, but predominantly from the North of England. The following centre's make up our children's services department:

Day Nursery and Children's Centre

Hillcrest Northern Counties Nursery has been established in response to the need expressed by parents of disabled children for a specialist all day nursery for babies from three months to five year old pre-school children. The nursery is one of the few in the country to operate on a fully integrated basis, with places for disabled children where the majority of children do not have disabilities.

Family Support Centre

The Percy Hedley Family Centre provides a range of activities to help parents and carers to work constructively with their children.

The concept of the Family Centre resulted from a small pilot scheme set up by the Foundation when a "School for Parents" was created. This facility has enabled parents to bring their pre-school children into the Foundation for practical help from specialist staff. Within the "School for Parents", parents and carers are encouraged to participate in group programmes, which involve children in activities specially designed to increase mobility and develop independence. These include sitting, standing, walking, manipulation and are based on the principles of Conductive Education.

The centre also has an information service that provides families with advice on benefits, placements, play schemes and other support organisations.

Foundation Schools

The Percy Hedley Foundation maintains two schools on three sites, Percy Hedley Primary Department in Forest Hall, Percy Hedley Secondary Department in Killingworth and Northern Counties School in Jesmond. The schools work with children aged six months to 19 years. Percy Hedley School specialises in working with three distinct groups of children. The work with children who have cerebral palsy is based on Conductive Education as practised at the Peto Institute in Budapest. Specialist teachers and therapists provide an integrated approach to working with children who have speech, language and communication difficulties. The school has considerable experience of working with children on the autistic spectrum. On the Northern Counties site, the school has a highly specialised educational provision for children with hearing impairment and additional disabilities, as well as for children with profound learning difficulties and additional sensory or health problems.

Adult Services

The Percy Hedley Foundation provides a full range of high quality, specialist services for disabled adults.

Residential Services

Residential accommodation at Chipchase House and Ferndene is in great demand and offers specialist high quality care. A range of living options include self-contained flats and en-suite rooms with shared communal facilities. Most of the residents have significant physical disabilities. The accommodation is organised on Person Centred principles and residents are enabled to access a wide range of activities both within the community and at Percy Hedley centres. This has been extended to include Tyne House and Moorview on the Northern Counties site in Jesmond.

Adult Day Services

Percy Hedley's Able2 Day Services are popular and widely recognised for the range of activities on offer. People have the opportunity to develop their skills in a range of activities – Horticulture, Ceramics, Art and Craft, Sport and Leisure, ICT, living skills and music. The Foundation also has a Business Park based 'Employability' Project offering work experience in ICT, marketing, design and print. A community base for disabled people has been opened at Linskill, North Shields.

Northern Counties College

Based in Jesmond, the FE college offers individualised learning for disabled students who would have significant difficulties in accessing other local further education colleges. Life skills, Adult and Community skills, Communication skills and Vocational and Employment skills are taught in this modern college, minutes from the heart of Newcastle.

Percy Hedley Academy for Disability Sport

The Academy aims to ensure all people have the opportunity to access sport regardless of their level of disability and of sporting ability. Although the Academy has purpose built facilities in Killingworth, it has a wider community role that means that it runs sporting activities in several centres throughout the North East.

Percy Hedley Patron Malcolm MacDonald with Daniel O'Brien and Michael Somerville.

Adult Conductive Education Centre

The centre has an innovative approach, adapting Conductive Education for use with adults who have acquired neurological conditions. This is proving highly popular and seems effective, although a research study still has to be completed that should, for the first time, provide evidence of its impact.

Letters received by Mr and Mrs Stephen Darke

On Thursday January 9th 1942 Mrs Molly Darke received this letter:-

"My Dear Martha

Cheers! Your trouble is over and a boy has come to make up for it all. May he never cause you another tear nor another moment's suffering. God bless you both."

> *Yours very sincerely*
> *Lawrence Campbell,*
> *St Theresa's Presbytery,*
> *Heaton Road,*
> *Newcastle upon Tyne 6*

On January 19th 1942 a second letter arrived from St Theresa's Presbytery:-

"My Dear Martha

Just ten days ago I wrote to congratulate and now I am writing to tell you to keep smiling. I still have hopes. Babies are wonderful and impossible to understand. But they and we are in God's hands. Don't forget that these are the loving hands of God and if He wants Stephen Lawrence in heaven now instead of later, how can we grumble. If God takes him you have someone of your very own in heaven to look after you instead of you looking after him in this world of woe.

But I still hope and so do you. Again, God bless you both."

> *Yours very sincerely*
> *L Campbell*

On April 5th 1948 Mr S F Darke, father of Stephen Lawrence, received the following letter from the Director of Education:-

"Dear Sir

I am to inform you that your son, Stephen, has been examined by one of my Committee's Assistant School Medical Officers and has been found to be educationally subnormal. So much so that it is felt that he will need special care and supervision. In these circumstances it has been decided to notify your son's name to the Local Mental Deficiency Authority. The purpose of this notification is to ensure that your son shall receive treatment and supervision suitable to his needs.

I am, however, to point out that you have the right to appeal against this proposal which must be exercised within fourteen days from the receipt of this letter. If you decide to appeal will you please write to the Ministry of Education, Special Services Branch, 15 Chesham Place, London SW1. You should, at the same time, notify me what action you have taken in the matter."

Yours faithfully
Director of Education, T Walling

A letter around the same time was received from the Special Services Branch, Ministry of Education, Belgrave Square, London SW1:-

"Sir

I am instructed by the Minister of Education to refer to the previous correspondence in the case of your son, Stephen Lawrence, and to state that, after careful consideration of all the evidence, he has directed in accordance with the proviso 57(3) of the Education 1944, that a report shall be issued to the Local Authority, that Stephen Lawrence Darke has been found incapable of receiving treatment at school."

I am, Sir, Your obedient servant

Following a reply to this correspondence which challenged the findings Stephen Darke (senior) received the following letter on April 28th 1948 from the Ministry of Education:-

"Sir

With reference to your letter of 17th April, I am directed by the Minister of Education to say that it is open to you, if you wish, to send to him a report signed by your doctor or other evidence in support of your contention that your son is not ineducable and that a report by the Local Education Authority to the Local Mental Deficiency Authority is not justified. It will be carefully considered with any reports which may be sent by the Local Education Authority.

If you wish to submit any evidence you should reply within fourteen days of the date of this letter."

I am, Sir, your obedient servant.

Stephen Darke responded by putting forward his case and firmly resisting a placement for his son in a mental institution. He went so far as to suggest an appropriate educational placement. His plea was rejected and in a letter dated October 15th 1948 he received the following reply:-

"Dear Sir

Mental Deficiency Act 1913-1938
Stephen Darke
I have to inform you that the hospital you mentioned to Dr Stephenson has been communicated with and the authorities thereat state that they do not take mentally defective children. I propose to bring this case before the committee on Friday, 22 October for a final decision as to the disposal of the child.
If you wish the child's name to be placed upon the waiting list for institutional care in an institution for mental defectives, please let us know before the day of the meeting."

Yours faithfully
Authorised Officer

Taken from newspaper cuttings

Big house sought for North East Spastics

The Friends of the Spastic Children (North East Area) are exploring Newcastle for suitable large house in which to establish their proposed school.

Following further discussions with Newcastle Education Authority it has been decided that control of the school will be in the hands of a voluntary board of managers.

The committee has agreed to house about 24 children as residents with a further 6 as day patients. Funds are gradually swelling and with the receipt of £148 from the Cinema Exhibition Association cash in hand totals more than £2416.

Film Show

To help parents and sympathisers to understand the work of such a school a film taken in Birmingham's school for spastic children has been obtained. This will be shown at Newgate House lecture hall above the New Theatre, Newcastle tomorrow (2.30 pm) to all interested.

After the show plans for the new school will be outlined by Mr G B Lauder, secretary.

He will inform his audience that the running costs will be provided by fees which the local education authorities will pay.

Grants for each child, which are agreed by the Ministry of Education, are £240 per year for day pupils and £350 a year for residents.

First children to attend will be selected from 180 spastic cases in Northumberland and Durham.

Unknown Donor backs school for spastics

With the promise of a donation from an anonymous subscriber, a school for the treatment and welfare of spastic children is likely to be established in Newcastle before the end of the year.

Preliminary plans for starting the school were discussed at a meeting of the executive committee of the Friends of Spastic Children (North East Area) today under the chairmanship of Mr Frank Wilkin. The film told a very moving story, not only concerning the children themselves but affecting the lives of the parents also.

Messrs Clarke Chapman's Concert Party's offer to help our funds was a spontaneous gesture due to a newspaper article and it may be that there are many other organisations and individuals who can help us if our problem is given publicity.

Geo. B Laudor, Honorary Secretary
Friends of the Spastic Children (NE Area)
22 Wingrove Gardens, Newcastle 4

It was decided to meet a special sub-committee of Newcastle Education Committee to discuss the control of the school. "We are now in a position financially to start the school", Mr G B Lauder, secretary of Friends of Spastic Children, told an Evening Chronicle representative. "We have sufficient funds with £3800 raised in 15 months".

Letter to Evening Chronicle

Sir – after a film shown by Friends of the Spastic Children (North East) in the Sanderson Orthopaedic Hospital the Lady Mayoress, Mrs V Grantham, consented to join our committee and the Lord Mayor (Councillor Charlton Curry) promised full support.

The search for a house in a suitable location was on. Simultaneously intense discussions about running costs and management structure were being debated. The key questions facing these early pioneers was who would shoulder the financial responsibilities? If the Local Authority accepted these then there were no worries. The Local Education Authority was quite keen whereas the Hospital Board dismissed the idea.

It had to be decided, in the event of the Local Education Authority running the school whether, firstly, children outside the immediate city would receive attention. Secondly, whether research aspects would receive efficient monitoring? Thirdly, would Sir James Spence be allowed the latitude he needed for research? His requirements were of considerable importance because he was very supportive of this effort and wished to be involved.

Appendices

The Babies Hospital

The Babies Hospital was the essence of achievement for Sir James Spence (Professor of Child Health 1928-1954) although he was not involved during the first six months when it first surfaced as a Day Nursery.

Miss Greta Rowell had spent her early life in Florence where she had run a small school for young children. She returned to her home in Newcastle at the beginning of World War I and was concerned at the number of children roaming the streets in the west end of the city while their mothers were making munitions in the local factories. In spite of her concern and her efforts to remedy this situation it was not until 1917 that she found a solution. She prevailed upon an old family friend to buy a house in which to provide one of the earliest day nurseries in the country.

After some researching a suitable house was found at 33 West Parade on the corner of Westmorland Road. The drains were in disrepair and appropriate equipment was needed. The benefactor, Mr Frederick Milburn gave an additional £500 to meet these costs. A seven man Committee was assembled and one, Mrs Coote was to give consistent service until 1944 when the Babies Hospital amalgamated with the Royal Victoria Infirmary. Miss Rowell was Honorary Secretary but she was much more than that. She gave her life and full attention to the little home, supervising every aspect of its work until her death in 1935. She kept all the minutes in her own handwriting and many make amusing reading today.

The first Matron, a state registered nurse, received a salary of £50 per annum plus £4 uniform and laundry allowance. Her assistant received £30 per annum and the only other staff member, a probationer, received £10 per annum. Together, they supervised 19 children. The mothers paid 6p a day (in decimal currency) to leave their children from 5.45 am until 7 pm but this was later reduced to 5p. The average cost per child per day was 22p. So it proved an ongoing struggle for the Committee to fund the deficit.

Support came eventually from the Newcastle Corporation, £50 was subscribed by the Newcastle Health Committee and the Medical Officer offered to supply goats milk free of charge. Domestic staff who broke any item of crockery were obliged to replace it. To boost the economy drive, at one stage unmarried mothers were employed and paid 5p per day for their surplus milk.

Dr Rutter, a General Practitioner on Westmorland Road, was the Medical Officer in charge of the Nursery. Following the examination of 146 children in 1918 he reported that while the children received love there was wholly inadequate attention to childcare and a high rate of diseases going unattended. It was Dr Rutter who reported in 1923 that a transition from Day Nursery to Babies Nursing Home was being realised. The Day Nursery attendance had fallen and there was an urgent need for this facility in Newcastle. The two main hospitals were fully occupied attending to serious cases.

The Babies Hospital up to this time had focused on feeding problems and training mothers in baby child care. It was at this stage that Dr James Spence became closely involved in this metamorphosis. Dr Spence was a man with a vision. He was both a physician and a teacher and all who came into contact with him benefited from his knowledge and observations. He was born, educated and lived in the North East and made a profound impact on the needs of children in the area during his lifetime. He was officially appointed Honorary Consulting Physician to the Babies Hospital. He saw patients twice a week; the number of beds was increased from 10 to 17 and in 1925 a room was adapted to accommodate mother and child so that the mother could be helped to establish a good breast feeding routine and receive guidance on child care under supervision. Eighty-six children were admitted in 1925 and the majority suffered from malnutrition. However, it was later discovered that most of these children had acute organic disease or infections. In the same year Dr Spence advised that a Consultant Surgeon should be appointed and so it was that the first operation for pyloric stenosis was performed. In his first annual report Dr Spence wrote, "The chief advantage in methods of treatment that we enjoy is in having available a daily supply of human milk from known and certified sources. This is kept for the severest cases, and the successful treatment of

Dr James Spence.

134

these can be attributed directly to the use of this human milk. In all cases the sources of the milk are under supervision and conveyed to the Nursery with suitable precautions. We feel that this is a feature of the work which needs special comment and emphasis, and its value is so evident that its use is sure to increase. Moreover, the method and organisation of the collection of human milk is, as far as is known, a new and unique step in England."

He pressed the Committee hard to purchase much needed equipment. By 1928 Mr W E M Wardell was appointed as Honorary Surgeon. Patient accommodation was in demand as admissions that year had risen to 110. It became apparent that the diagnoses were often ill-defined and Miss Rowell became increasingly alarmed at the number with infections but recognised that their needs must be met. The Babies Hospital was giving a historic lead in this area of paediatric medicine.

Scientific aspects of the work were undertaken by Dr A F Bernard Shaw who was subsequently appointed Professor of Pathology at the Royal Victoria Infirmary. Nursing staff increased so that by 1926 there was a matron, three staff nurses and eight probationers. One, Sister Curry had a severe hearing loss but in spite of this she was described as having unique nursing qualities, skilful handling of very sick babies and compassion. She remained at the hospital for fifteen years.

In 1926 medical students began to attend the outpatient clinics. Postgraduates attended classes officially organised through the University. The major concerns were centred on tuberculosis in infancy, and the increasing number of cases of pyloric stenosis. The work load for Mr Wardell was expanding and included correction of hare lip and cleft palates. This became an important aspect of the work of the hospital.

An important landmark arose when it was agreed that the postoperative daily care of babies and infants should be undertaken by paediatric physicians. Such a change in attitude was unique and the result of the professional cooperation between Mr Wardell and Dr Spence which gave rise to the present day recognised role of the Paediatrician.

Further expansion of services and accommodation necessitated finding more rooms. In 1932 the Committee bought the house next door. Until now mothers and babies had been admitted for short periods to deal with breast feeding problems but account had to be taken of hospitalisation for other conditions and the associated problems which arose through separation of mother and child.

A policy was adopted whereby mothers were admitted so that they could assist in nursing their own child and it proved to have untold advantages for all those involved.

The house next door was a real success and so prompted even further expansion and this was beginning to cause Miss Rowell a fair degree of distress when discussions of an amalgamation between the Royal Victoria Infirmary, Newcastle and a newly built Children's Hospital were proposed. The new hospital was to be on the Castle Leazes site and so combine the Babies Hospital and the children's wards of the Royal Victoria Infirmary. She feared a loss of identity: a loss of character if the Babies Hospital became engulfed by this larger hospital. She was increasingly concerned that attention to acutely ill children and scientific research detracted from the needs of healthy children and prevention of disease. The amalgamation was not adopted, the character and style were retained.

Miss Rowell died in 1935 and Dr Spence described her as one who had demonstrated diligence and foresight; a lady of quality who had demonstrated a most sympathetic understanding of the needs of the mothers and children of the City of Newcastle.

Following Miss Rowell's death the Babies Hospital continued to expand and yet another neighbouring house was bought and the numbers increased.

1939 brought the threat of war and with it the threat to children's safety due to the proximity of the Elswick works of Vickers-Armstrong which rendered them and all staff particularly vulnerable. In 1820 Lady Ridley had built a large nursery wing at Blagdon Hall. There were ten rooms either side of a long corridor for her ten children with a nursery at the end, an ideal site for relocation of the Babies Hospital. Consultations took place with the Ministry of Health and it was agreed that Blagdon Hall was suitable for the evacuation but they were not to go before a telegram was received to give the go ahead. As this did not arrive they did not hang around and departed on September 1st. Estate workers together with the members of Stannington Women's Institute had rallied to prepare for this transformation involving much scrubbing and cleaning. On September 1st 1939 all equipment was transported to Blagdon. Nurses and babies followed in cars driven by the Committee members.

All and everything was there by lunchtime in a considerable muddle. Mr Cowell, the appointed surgeon at the time arrived with a very sick baby requiring immediate surgery. Lady Ridley sterilised the instruments in a kettle on the kitchen fire and Mr Cowell operated on the baby on a bath rack across the bath. The baby came to no harm and recovered well. From hereon Lady Ridley became the surgeon's assistant because nurses were unavailable due to call up for military service. In spite of her initial inexperience she spent the next five years preparing the converted bathroom/operating theatre and assisting in the operations. The outpatients continued to attend West Parade and a few beds were retained there for emergencies. Between 1939 and 1944 more than three hundred mothers stayed at Blagdon Hall. When in 1943 the Chair of Child Health was created, Dr James Spence was appointed the first Professor of Paediatrics in England. It led to the transfer of the Outpatient Department at West Parade into the Children's Clinic at the Royal Victoria Infirmary. West Parade then continued as it had begun as a day nursery.

The creation of the Babies Hospital made a marked contribution to hospital planning as well as influencing attitudes to improve the conditions for mother and child. All of which was due to the vision of Professor James Spence.

The Babies Hospital, 33 West Parade, Newcastle.

The W J Sanderson Orthopaedic Hospital School

This hospital school was situated on Salters Road, Gosforth and has now been demolished. In 1887 a noble organisation, the Prudhoe Street Mission reported sending 'five little cripples to homes in London'. This information highlighted the need for a similar facility in Newcastle and so it came about that Mr W J Sanderson, a well-known philanthropist, set in motion a process and provided the means to rectify this situation.

William John Sanderson

William John Sanderson was the son of a wine and spirit merchant and joined the business in 1870. By 1887 he retired from the store to devote his time to philanthropic projects. He was educated at Bruce's School, Percy Street, Newcastle and at Harrogate.

He became a JP for Newcastle and Northumberland and lived at Eastfield Hall, Warkworth. When W J Sanderson became Lord Mayor of Newcastle he lived in the Mansion House. He guaranteed the rent of a house 'Fellside' Whickham as well as meeting the cost of furniture and equipment. Six destitute children were admitted there in 1888. Owing to the demand for such facilities quickly the number rose to twelve and so 'The Cripples Home' moved to the Red House, Wallsend Green in 1889 which had accommodation for fifty children. The object of the home, it was claimed, was to "clothe, feed and shelter the crippled children of the Northern Counties, to educate and teach them trades in order that they may be better equipped to undertake the battle of life, and further utilise the orthopaedic treatment, that miracle of modern science, to alleviate the sufferings and in many cases to cure these poor crippled and deformed little ones."

The Red House provided a large garden at the back where the children could play and the house had about twenty rooms. When the coal industry was at a peak and Wallsend was flourishing, the Red House was considered to be one of the best bordering onto the Green. It was noted that once admitted the general health of the children improved.

The demand for places gathered momentum. In 1893 a 'Fancy Fair' raised a sum of £1600 which allowed for the purchase of two acres of land at Gosforth, a suburb of the city

138

of Newcastle. By 1896 building began and by 1897 the Cripples Home moved to Gosforth where it was now possible to accommodate one hundred children.

Mrs W J Sanderson laid the foundation stone on June 12th 1896 before a large gathering of influential city dignitaries. The formal opening of the home took place on September 30th 1897. Mr Hilton Philipson and his family had shown great interest in this project and had made generous donations. When his widow Mrs Hilton Philipson opened the home she was

" The Red House," Wallsend.

presented with a gold key by Mr W J Sanderson as a memento of the occasion and said, "In the name of the Committee I beg of you Mrs Philipson, to declare this home open, in the hope that many sufferers will find relief therein, and that these doors may never be closed to any poor crippled child needing succour or help."

The move to Gosforth allowed the provision of elementary education as well as technical training for boys in tailoring, shoe making and gardening. For the girls their training was in dressmaking, cooking and domestic work.

On July 3rd 1908 the Prince and Princess of Wales, later to become King George V and Queen Mary, paid a visit. By this time Mr W J Sanderson had become the Lord Mayor of Newcastle. Their expressions of sympathy with this particular charity proved very gratifying for the people of the North. The following week they consented to becoming patrons of the Home.

Forty years after renting 'Fellside' Whickham the introduction of orthopaedics emerged. In 1917 Sir Robert Jones, an eminent Orthopaedic Surgeon of the time visited the home and went on to claim that 90% of the children could be cured by surgery. Based on this recommendation a ward was made available in the Home for Incurables at Spital Tongues under the guidance of Professor Rutherford Morison. An interest was stimulated in the use of orthopaedic surgery and correction of deformities but it should be stressed that the majority of these deformities were the result of rickets, tuberculosis and poliomyelitis.

These facilities were further developed with the opening of the Orthopaedic Hospital as part of the Home for Crippled Children in Gosforth on a second visit by Sir Robert Jones on February 15th 1924. The Duke of Northumberland occupied the chair and spoke of the advances in surgery during and since World War I, never more so than in orthopaedic procedures. He went on to congratulate the Committee on enlisting the support of Sir Robert Jones whom he described as 'the greatest living authority on the science of orthopaedics' at that time.

The claims being made for successes, while undoubtedly appropriate for those children with physical abnormalities, there remained much to learn about surgical procedures for children with cerebral palsy. Professor Rutherford Morison who began the work at Spital Tongues recognised the advantages of orthopaedics but made clear that a long period of rehabilitation, well considered and managed would ultimately determine the outcome. This consisted of re-education, physical training, massage and electrical stimulation.

In recognition of the contribution made by W J Sanderson a portrait was commissioned and painted by Mr T B Garvie. It was presented to him at the 37th Annual Meeting of the home on Armistice Day, November 11th 1925. The President, Sir Francis D Blake said, "It is a fine thing when a man of position gives his life's work to such a cause as this. He has given his money without stint, but what is better still he has given his loving care to the children who have found a safe home within these walls." At the same time it was agreed that there should be a change of name to the W J Sanderson Home for Crippled Children.

On Friday May 28th 1926, HRH Duke of York, who later became George VI, visited the home. As he was leaving a toy cloth rabbit made in the home was placed in his car with an inscription stating that it was a gift to the baby Princess from the Crippled Children's Home. It was unimaginable at the time that she would become Elizabeth II.

During World War II the home and the hospital were evacuated to Meldon Hall where the average length of stay steadily decreased. By the time of the return to Gosforth the average length of stay was 21 days. By 1946 rickets could be prevented by vitamin D, tuberculosis could be treated by antibiotics and poliomyelitis could be prevented by vaccination. Orthopaedics provided solutions for children with physical problems but none of this met the needs of the neurologically impaired children.

The Cripples Home and the Day Nursery 'Fellside' Whickham experienced in their history, changes of emphasis. Both in their particular way created conditions, codes of practice, a culture and a combined knowledge which was used to advantage in the creation of the Percy Hedley School and Clinic in 1953.

The W J Sanderson Orthopaedic Hospital School before demolition.

Biographies

All biographies taken from Percy Foundation archives.

Sir James Spence Kt MC MD LLD Hons DSc FRCP, Professor of Child Health 1928 – 1954

James Spence was born at Amble, on the Northumberland Coast, in 1892 into a secure Victorian family. His father was an architect. His early school years were passed in Newcastle and York and from hereon he became a student at the College of Medicine in Newcastle. During his student years he played centre half for the University football team and was a member of the Officers' Training Corps. In 1914 he qualified with an honours degree. Very soon he was enlisted into the army and posted to a field ambulance in a new division and remained with the same unit until the end of the war.

Almost five years after qualification he returned to civilian medicine and became a House Physician at the Royal Victoria Infirmary, Newcastle. He moved on to become Casualty Officer at the Hospital for Sick Children, Great Ormond Street, London. His next post was at St Thomas's Hospital followed by a period in Glasgow. In 1921, he took the membership of the Royal College of Physicians and returned to Newcastle in 1922 where he was appointed Medical Registrar and Clinical Pathologist at the Infirmary.

Between 1922 and 1928 James Spence was very busy acquiring knowledge of the state of health of children in the Newcastle area and the development of the unique Babies Hospital as it was developed from a wartime nursery.
In 1928 he was appointed as an Honorary Assistant Physician on the staff of the Infirmary and this was the beginning of Consultant practice in general medicine. This appointment did not interfere with his work at the Babies Hospital or his interest in a small group of people concerned about child welfare.

In 1942 the Nuffield Trustees offered to establish a Chair of Child Health in the University of Durham but situated in the Royal Victoria Infirmary. This was the first such chair in England and Wales. James Spence was appointed and held this position until his early death in 1954.

Professor James Spence travelled widely and made valuable contacts at home and abroad. His knowledge and experience were much in demand. As a result he was involved in many advisory committees.

In 1950 Professor James Spence received his Knighthood in recognition of his diligent work and his determination to draw full attention to paediatric medicine and involvement of the family. The following year he became President of the British Paediatric Association which he had helped to found.

Professor Donald Court
1912 – 1994

Seymour Donald Maynard Court was born in Wem, Shropshire, on 4th January 1912. He began his career in dentistry but after 3 years changed to the medical course qualifying in the Birmingham Medical School in 1936. From thereon he worked at Great Ormond Street and the Children's Department at Westminster Hospital and after that in the Emergency Medical Service. In 1946 he moved to Newcastle upon Tyne to undertake research in the developing Department of Child Health led by Professor James Spence. A research project was being designed – The Thousand Family Study, which followed a thousand babies born in Newcastle and continued to report at intervals on their development – physical, social and psychological. Between 1947 and 1954 he visited thousands of homes. This challenging experience enabled him to formulate his plans to develop Child Health Services.

In 1950 Donald Court was appointed Reader in Child Health. On the death of Sir James Spence he succeeded to the Chair of Child Health in 1955. He was committed to teaching and had a high regard for students treating them with respect. He retired from the Chair and his clinical work in 1972 to become President of the British Paediatric Association. His ideas were developed in 'Paediatrics in the Seventies' after which he was invited to chair a government committee to review the Child Health Services. In the 1980s following his retirement Professor Court was interested and involved with the introduction of Conductive Education in the Percy Hedley nursery. He died on 4th September 1994.

Dr Errington Ellis MA, MD (Cantab) FRPCH, DCH
Medical Director, Percy Hedley Centre, 1921 – 2006

Errington Ellis was born in Gosforth in 1921. At the age of 11 an older brother, aged 15, died of meningococcal meningitis and this had a profound effect upon him and his family. This subsequently influenced him to study medicine.

He was educated at Rugby School then at Gonville and Caius College, Cambridge and finally St Bartholomew's Hospital, London. He qualified in 1945 and after working for six months as a House Physician he was called up into the RAF for National Service. For two years he worked in an RAF hospital attached to a Recruit Centre where there was a high incidence of streptococcal infection and consequently of rheumatic fever. Following demobilisation he returned to St Bartholomew's Hospital as a Supernumerary Registrar in the Children's Department. Eventually, he returned to Newcastle as Registrar in the Department of Child Health directed by Sir James Spence. This Department was at the centre of a rapidly developing service for a regional population of three million. He was at that time particularly responsible to Dr Donald Court. It was from thereon in the early fifties that he gained broad experience but came to realise that he did not enjoy the drama of acute medicine and surgery and that his real interest lay in the special aspects of disease.

Sir James Spence used to float in front of his registrars a number of job opportunities in his rapidly expanding department. He discouraged Errington Ellis from entering general practice; instead he appointed him First Assistant in his department and delegated three areas of work: the Thousand Families Survey, Medical Officer to the Royal Grammar School and charge of the Newcastle centre of a UK/US multicentre study of cortisone in the treatment of rheumatic fever.

Sir James Spence had been invited to become Chairman of the Medical Advisory Committee for the Parents' Association of Friends of the Spastic Children (North East Area) and in December 1952 he had a list of 300 children with cerebral palsy. He presented Errington Ellis with the task of organising full detailed assessment of each over a three week period.

Between 1953 – 1971 babies and children of all ages with suspected motor impairment were seen in the Percy Hedley Clinic for assessment. Following consultation and advice from Donald Court, Professor of Child Health, Dr Errington Ellis continued to expand his clinical role based now in the Department of Child Health, RVI, Newcastle. The Child Development Centre opened in 1971 in purpose built accommodation and from thereon Dr Errington Ellis continued his role at Percy Hedley School as visiting consultant and expanded his teaching role in the hospital.

Errington Ellis felt privileged to have had massive support early in his career from Sir James Spence and latterly from Professor Donald Court who arranged for him to be appointed as a Consultant Paediatrician and as a lecturer jointly in the Department of Child Health and in the Department of Family & Community Medicine.

Throughout his working life he maintained contact with and interest in Educational and Social Services. He was Chairman of the Governors of a private school and of an approved school and Chairman of the Community Paediatric Group of the British Paediatric Association.

Errington Ellis was truly a family man and with the support of his wife, Alysoun, he cared for his own four children and was unstinting in the time and attention he devoted to children and adults with cerebral palsy and their families. He worked tirelessly to foster and promote the development of the Percy Hedley Centre as a holistic interdisciplinary organisation.

Following retirement in 1985 he enjoyed long days working in the garden of the family cottage situated between the North Northumberland beaches and the Cheviot Hills. Always interested in DIY he was kept occupied in helping his children to establish their own homes and in helping to care for six grandchildren. Between times he enjoyed walking and studying industrial history.

Dr Errington Ellis died on 28th July 2006.

Muriel Elizabeth Morley 1899 – 1993

Muriel Morley was born on February 20th 1899. In 1920 she graduated with a degree in physics and biology and for the next ten years she taught physics to fifth and sixth formers. After a visit to India she developed a chronic illness and returned home and was uncertain about her future. In 1932 she answered an unusual advertisement. William Wardell, a Newcastle Surgeon had developed a new type of pharyngoplasty for cleft palates and was seeking 'an educated woman' who would assess the children's speech before and after surgery.

Muriel Morley was duly appointed and became fascinated by this work. Her first book 'Cleft Palate and Speech' was published in 1945. In 1939 she was appointed as speech therapist at the Royal Victoria Infirmary, Newcastle and eventually established a clinic there. Shortly afterwards James Spence was appointed Professor of Child Health. Donald Court came to Newcastle in 1947 as Reader in Child Health and was encouraged by Sir James Spence to take an interest in Muriel Morley's work. She worked closely with him as first reader and when he became Professor of Child Health. She worked also with Henry Miller, Professor of Neurology and Roger Garside, Reader in Applied Psychology. Joint weekly meetings were held when a wide range of children with speech and language disorders were seen.

It became apparent that there was a need to establish a department of speech and this was acknowledged by the professors of all the relevant disciplines. Britain's first university department of speech was founded in 1959. For six years she edited the Journal of the College of Speech Therapists and became its third president.

Muriel Morley was also concerned with the foundation of the Percy Hedley Centre and held the post of Chairman of the School Governors for many years and chiefly responsible for the setting up of the adult section with its workshop and hostel.

Frank W Wilkin Esq, T D
Chairman 1950 – 1961

In December 1949 the first meeting was called 'for the establishment of a spastic unit' in the North East. Mr Frank Wilkin was listed amongst those who attended. He was a business man and the father of a cerebral palsied child. This was the start of a mammoth task facing an enthusiastic band of parents of cerebral palsied children frustrated by the lack of educational and therapeutic facilities to meet their needs. Frank Wilkin was elected Chairman in March 1950 and this was the beginning of a long connection with the Percy Hedley Centre. Although a parent of a son with cerebral palsy Mr Wilkin did not benefit as his son was too old for admission to the school. However, he had a strong desire to help children of the future and their families and as he was well known in business life on Tyneside, he was able to call on all his friends and associated for support. He resigned from the Committee in

1959 and was unanimously elected President which enabled him to maintain a less exacting contact with the work. His interest in the progress of the Centre never wavered until his death on 25th April 1976.

Herbert H Severs
1953 – 1965

Harry Severs was one of the key figures in the founding of the Percy Hedley Centre. He was born in 1889 in Crossgate, Leeds. His family moved to Cheshire where he received his early education. After matriculation at Stockport Grammar School in 1906 he became a pupil teacher for two years before embarking on teacher training at Chester College from 1908 – 1910. He had a natural flair and wide-ranging scholarship which made him a teacher of great distinction.

From 1910 Harry taught in schools at Bramhall and Poynton. In 1920 he took up a post at Mobberley Open Air School for Manchester Boys. It was from here he came to the North East in 1931 as Headmaster of the W J Sanderson Orthopaedic Hospital School in Gosforth.

He was a small dapper man, always neatly dressed wearing a bow tie. He gained great respect from his pupils and was intimately involved with the teaching and recognised the importance of developing the personality, the importance of codes of conduct and social skills.

During this period he became increasingly aware of the particular needs of the child with cerebral palsy. While attending a Ministry of Education course at King's College London in 1947 he discussed his concerns with Miss I Dunsdon who was at that time gathering data about cerebral palsy for the National Foundation of Education Research and who was later in 1952 to publish an influential book, 'The Educability of Cerebral Palsied Children'.

After discussing his ideas with Mr Donald Brown FRCS who had recently been appointed Medical Officer of the Sanderson Orthopaedic Hospital they decided to work towards the creation of a special unit for spastic children. Their enthusiasm was shared by Mr George Lauder, father of a cerebral palsied son who set about harnessing help of other parents.

Harry presented the idea for a separate block of classrooms within the hospital grounds to serve the special needs of cerebral palsied children to the School Managers in 1948.

These efforts resulted in a special section for spastic children using the newly built assembly hall and thus laying the foundation for the Percy Hedley Centre for Spastics.

Under the chairmanship of Mr Frank Wilkin, Harry became Honorary Secretary of the Friends of Spastic Children, North East Area in 1951. In August of that year their funds stood at £2000. Through the efforts of Mr Douglas Pool, one of the Trustees of the Percy Hedley Trust, a grant of £5,500 enabled Hampeth Lodge in Forest Hall to be purchased.

In 1952 Harry resigned his Headship of the Sanderson Orthopaedic Hospital School. From thereon he devoted his time and attention to the administration of the Percy Hedley Centre. Until the Centre was opened his home in Fern Avenue, Jesmond was the registered office of the charity. For the next thirteen years he directed his energies into fundraising, promoting the centre to the public as well as administration. Harry retired in 1965 although he continued to serve on the Centre's committees for many years after this. He was a modest man who achieved much in his lifetime but refused any public acknowledgement for his work. When he relinquished his post as Secretary he said, "My greatest reward is seeing this Centre firmly established and running well."

He died in December 1982 a few days short of his 93rd birthday.

Mrs E M Cauldwell, First Headteacher
1953 - 1963

Molly Cauldwell was appointed as the first Headteacher at the school in 1953. She had taught previously a small group of children with cerebral palsy in the W J Sanderson Orthopaedic Hospital School. At the same time, Hilda Shield and Molly Cooknell, two teachers who had worked there with her joined the staff. Also, Mr Harry Severs, retired Headmaster who was Chief Administrator.

Molly Cauldwell was the widow of the Rev J D Cauldwell, Vicar of Cambo and later of Mitford and mother of three grown up children at the time of her appointment.

She was daughter of Rev E I Fripp who was a Shakespearean scholar. After teacher training at the Mather Training College Manchester she received a first class certificate of the National Froebel Union. She joined the staff of the demonstration school attached to the college and later taught at the Queen Elizabeth School for Girls, Barnet. In the early years of the war she ran a boarding and day school for evacuee children at Mitford Vicarage. Her other interests included the Women's Institute and Guiding. She served on the Northumberland Executive Committee for the Women's Institute and was a Girl Guides Commissioner for the Morpeth Division.

Molly Cauldwell remained in post for ten years and during that first decade made a valuable contribution to the development, the organisation and the atmosphere within the school.

Mrs Hilda J Shield MBE
1953 - 1977

Hilda Shield was born in Belford in 1917. She was educated at Berwick and started her teaching career in September 1937. After gaining a wide and varied experience in infant and junior schools she joined the staff of the Sanderson Orthopaedic School in 1950. It was here she met and taught her first cerebral palsied pupils. When the Percy Hedley School opened on January 1st 1953 it was a natural progression that she should be appointed as the Deputy Headteacher. For the next twenty four years she devoted herself wholly to furthering the interest of the school. Her outstanding contribution to special education was recognised by the award of MBE in the New Year's Honours List of 1969. Following retirement Hilda continued her active association in the affairs of the School and was appointed to serve on the School Management Committee. Hilda died in January 2011.

David Dorman Johnston
1963 – 1986

David Johnston was appointed Head Teacher in 1963 following the retirement of Mrs Molly Cauldwell and he held this post until 1986.

He was born in Linthouse, Glasgow – a fairly poor area of tenements, shipyards and factories. He was the youngest of eight children, two of whom died – one in infancy and another at the age of 12. At the age of 2 he was accidentally shot in one eye by his elder brother. David opened a door into a room where his brother had set up a dart board on the back and just at the point when a rubber dart was being fired. This incident resulted in a long period of hospitalisation which he remembered most vividly and, in spite of regular visits to the

Eye Department, he never regained full vision in his left eye. Total blindness was predicted and initially a special school placement was recommended whereby he would be educated alongside children with severe learning difficulties. His father fought vigorously against the idea and he was educated at Govan School Glasgow. Aged 18 he embarked on an MA at Glasgow University and, after serving in the Second World War, at the age of 23 he returned there and got a first class Honours in an Ed.B which focused mainly on psychology. This was followed by one year Teacher Training and then a B.Ed at Durham University. The latter was conducted externally and focused on preparation of his thesis – 'Juvenile Delinquency – The History of Approved Schools'.

For 3 years David Johnston served in the RAF. Owing to the defect in his left eye he was recruited to Codes and Cyphers. He was selected for special training at Sir John Cass Institute in London and eventually responsible for encoded and deciphered messages to the Governor General, Lord Louis Mountbatten and his staff in Delhi. As well as Delhi he worked in Madras and Ceylon (Sri Lanka). It had been planned for him to be landed on Japanese shores for further assignments but these were aborted after the dropping of the atomic bomb.

After the war he taught "difficult boys" in mainstream school for two years then moved to Thornley Park Approved School situated on the outskirts of Paisley. In 1953 he was invited to apply for the post of Deputy Head Teacher at Netherton Approved School which lies near Stannington Village, 4 miles south of Morpeth. Here he lived and worked long hours with responsibility for boys aged 15 – 18 years over a period of 10 years.

In 1963 he was invited to apply for the Headship of the Percy Hedley School. In spite of lack of knowledge of cerebral palsy he was appointed and proved to be a quick learner. Later he lectured on this subject in the UK, Germany, USA and Canada. In 1969 he won a Churchill Fellowship and studied aspects of cerebral palsy in the USA and Toronto.

For 22 years David Johnston lived and worked on the premises and raised a family of 3 sons. All were unstinting in their time devoted to involvement in extra curricular activities for the children. These included scouting, camping and sports. He retired in 1986 and until his death in 2005 many old pupils kept in regular touch with him and his wife.

He was a keen photographer, an adventurous traveller and

had a great interest in the English language.

David Johnston had many friends. He was a good communicator, fair-minded, perceptive with a good sense of humour. These attributes combined with his academic ability contributed greatly to the high standards, the inter-disciplinary harmony and co-operation which have been fostered and are in evidence to this day.

"Last Christmas I was struck by the picture of a rather fierce looking grey-haired Scotsman with an untidy moustache carrying a very small baby down the corridor in his arms. Mrs Atkinson could only bring Stephen to the Outpatients' party if she could also bring her new baby with her. It was noisy in the dining hall and David Johnston wanted to find somewhere quiet for the baby to sleep. "Gosh!" I thought, "that man's come a long way in a short time. All the way from a Senior Approved School dealing with 17 and 18 year old toughs, where he was renowned for his fair but strict discipline, to the tenderness with which he handled that new born baby.

Not only has he learnt a great deal about brain injured children, but he has taught us about child care and special education. The Percy Hedley School has changed out of all recognition in the past 5 years. He has been responsible for many of the changes and has held us together and led us through these turbulent times".

Dr Errington Ellis, 16th Anniversary 1969

"It is a great privilege to be a teacher – and a big responsibility. It has been a great privilege to have been a teacher at Percy Hedley School. During my time here (22 years 1963-1985) exactly 400 children have been admitted. I hope I have been of some service to them."

David D Johnston

David Johnston died in 2005.

Rosemary Pattison, Deputy Headteacher 1977 – 1991

Rosemary Pattison was born in Scarborough and as her father was serving in the armed forces in World War II the family moved around to Bury, York and Burton-on-Trent. Eventually she settled back in Scarborough where she attended the Scarborough Convent as a boarder. From there she moved to Croydon to embark on her 3 year teacher training. The final year was spent at Whickham Court, Froebel Foundation, Kent where she gained the National Teaching Certificate. Her first post (1952 – 55) was residential at Solefield Preparatory School for 7 – 8 year olds at Sevenoaks, Kent. After three years she moved North to take up a post in Newcastle at the Church High Junior School. She was employed there from 1955 – 1961 and was married during that time. For the following eight years she was at home raising two young sons. It was 1969 when she was approached by the Local Education Authority to take up a part-time post teaching mixed ESN children, eight to ten years at Blakelaw Special School where she remained from 1969 – 1971.

A call came from a friend, Dorothy Jamieson, who was domestic science teacher at the Percy Hedley School. She had been asked by David Johnston if she knew of anyone suitably trained for remedial teaching. Rosemary responded when she received a call from David Johnston. "Can you come in for a cup of tea and a chat?" She had an informal interview with Hilda Shield, the Deputy Head, and David Johnston. From thereon she was a part-time remedial teacher in the school from 1971 – 1974. Following the premature death of her husband she became employed full time from 1974 – 1977. Hilda Shield was retiring in 1977 and Rosemary was invited to take the post of Deputy Headteacher following a very brief informal interview with Hilda Shield, Dr Ellis and David Johnston. Until her retirement in 1991 she continued with limited remedial teaching but her responsibilities were broad and varied. She was manager of auxiliary staff. She organised student placement, managed the budget for requisition of school equipment and furniture, selected the décor and deputised in the absence of the Headteacher.

Her role was flexible and varied and included the management of care staff. Her contribution to the success of the Integrated Education programme introduced in 1980 proved invaluable.

Jim Ferris OBE, B.A., MSc., C.Psychol
1986 - 2008

Jim Ferris arrived at Percy Hedley as Head Teacher in 1985, and became the Foundation's Chief Executive in 1995. He began his career as a teacher thirty-six years ago, the last thirty in special education and caring for people with special needs as a Care Worker, Teacher, Psychologist, Head Teacher and Chief Executive. He has served on numerous bodies, including the Health Authority, the Scottish Office, Cerebral Palsy Ireland and was Chair of the UK Federation for Conductive Education for three years in the 1990s.

Arriving at the Percy Hedley Foundation in 1985, he was struck by the school's unique qualities, its specialism, its professionalism, and the integrated approach to therapy and education. His vision was to develop these qualities further, and to secure the school's reputation regionally, nationally and internationally. The visit of HRH The Princess of Wales in 1989 cemented that recognition. The school continued to develop and expand. By 1995, it had a record number of pupils, the nursery and primary departments of the school had been rebuilt, and a new boarding unit provided the highest quality care, short breaks and adventure weekends for pupils.

In 1995, he became the Percy Hedley Foundation's first Chief Executive, with a vision to initiate the same quality of provision within Adult Services. The past ten years have seen a positive explosion of development for adults and children. Developments for adults include a social activity centre opened by HRH The Duke of York, a unique covered street of bungalows, a major refurbishment of the Day Centre to provide a wide range of Day Care Services, including an ICT suite, music studio, multi sensory rooms, horticultures, living skills, outdoor pursuits and physiotherapy. Developments for children have included a new secondary school, which was opened by HRH Princess Alexandra, a post-16 centre, a Family Support Service and a School for Parents.

The Foundation's goal is to 'promote the rights, needs and aspirations of people with disabilities'. To this end, it continues to listen to children, families and adults, and to develop the services they want and need.

As well as Chief Executive Officer, Jim Ferris operated as one of the Foundation's Developmental & Educational Psychologists. He retired in August 2008.

In 2009 he was awarded an OBE for services to local and national Special Needs Education.

Ester Cotton
1912 – 2003
Ester Cotton was born in Copenhagen. She was one of five children whose father was a mathematician and headmaster of a school. After training as a gymnast she went on to study remedial gymnastics in Germany. In 1934 she came to England and studied physiotherapy and eventually held the

superintendent physiotherapist post at the Maudsley Hospital followed by that at the Royal Richmond Hospital.

In 1959 Ester joined Dr and Mrs Bobath at the Western Cerebral Palsy Centre, London where she received training and became a senior tutor. Following a visit to Budapest and a meeting with Professor Andras Peto at the Institute for the Motor Disordered in 1965 she embarked on a long crusade to introduce the Conductive Education System in the UK. For the next 25 years she worked tirelessly, running courses on Conductive Education in many countries. As a result of her generosity, charisma and teaching ability she made many friends who had little difficulty understanding her message. She was dedicated to her work and was able to ride over many obstacles and disappointments with dignity when she tried to organise Conductive Education in the UK.

She was appointed Physiotherapy Advisor for the Spastics' Society (SCOPE) and in 1986 was awarded a fellowship by The Chartered Society of Physiotherapy. In 1990 Ester was given the Honorary Conductor award by The Peto Institute in Budapest and in 1992 an Honorary Doctor Degree from Queen Margaret's College, Edinburgh.

Olive Surtees
1959 - 1992

Olive Surtees was born on 17th March 1931 in Appleby-in-Cumbria. After early education in the local church school she became a boarder at Oakfield School, Kirby Lonsdale in 1941. In 1949 she embarked on physiotherapy training at the Royal Victoria Infirmary, Newcastle and in 1952 accepted a full time post at the W J Sanderson Orthopaedic Hospital School. In 1953 she moved to work at the Royal Infirmary, Preston, Lancashire. On return to Newcastle in 1956, following her marriage, she worked in the General Hospital, Sunderland until the birth of her first child in 1958. In 1959 she was accepted for a part-time basic grade post at the Percy Hedley School which was increased to full time by 1964 after her second child was born. Between 1960 -1978 she received valuable childcare and domestic help from Mrs Suzie Crozier, the mother of Ronnie who was one of the first Percy Hedley pupils.

In 1974, sponsored by the Foundation, she completed the one year Open University course "A Handicapped Person in the Community". In 1979 she was appointed Head of

Physiotherapy and throughout the next ten years, in conjunction with David Johnston, Jim Ferris and other Heads of Departments, steered conductive education practice in the school.

Following her retirement in 1992 she acted as a part-time consultant at the Hormsey Centre for Conductive Education in London for seven years. Supported mainly by the charity British Executive Service Overseas she covered 42 assignments in Poland between 1992 and 2006. Supported by the International Cerebral Palsy Society she accompanied Anita Loring, Secretary General and Carol Hughes, retired Headteacher on assignments in Greece, Lebanon and Nepal.

Nora Valentine Culloty
1952 – 1975

Val Culloty was appointed as the first Superintendent Physiotherapist at the Percy Hedley School in October 1952. From this base she assisted in the development of services for many others in different strategic locations in five Northern Counties.

She came from Co Kerry and trained in Birmingham and had been working in an orthopaedic clinic in Wallasey. Undoubtedly, she was a woman with a strong pioneering spirit and an ideal choice for a small professional team. She completed the Bobath training in London, a training recognised at that time as the most comprehensive and most appropriate for the treatment of motor disorders. From thereon all her staff were expected to do likewise and this postgraduate training was financed by the School.

Over time Val Culloty built up a strong physiotherapy department fostering continuous professional development and harmonious interdisciplinary teamwork within the school. She was involved with many people in the UK and abroad who were spearheading similar projects at that time and co-arranged many courses in the school for the benefit of others. She produced a useful handbook, The Hemiplegic Child' published by 'SCOPE' in 1964.

Val Culloty was modest, dedicated and never sought public recognition. She was the catalyst which engendered a style of management and professionalism which has been upheld to this day. She made an immeasurable contribution to the development of the Percy Hedley School.

Val Culloty died in 2002.

Head of Departments in 1993. Back row, left to right: Jenny Buckle, John Bloomfield, Richard Barron, Stewart Evans, Hazel Howliston, Raymond O'Dowd. Front row: Marian Farmer, Lynne Birrell, Jim Ferris, Anne Coates and Alice Fee.

David Johnston and Colin Coates in 1982.

Bibliography

Johnson, D D
Year Book 1983-84
Percy Hedley Foundation

Miller, J F W
Sir James Spence Kt MC MD LLD Durham Hons DSc FRCP,
Professor of Child Health (1928-1954)
Journal of Medical Biography Physicians 1997; 5:1-7

Percy Hedley Foundation
Celebrating 50 Years of Achievement
Percy Hedley Foundation

Ridley, U
The Babies Hospital, Newcastle upon Tyne
Andrew Reid & Company, Newcastle upon Tyne

A History of the W J Sanderson Orthopaedic Hospital School
Commemorative Publication 1926

The photograph of the Babies Hospital on page 137 is courtesy of the West Newcastle Picture History Collection.

The Percy Hedley Foundation

Tomorrow, with your support
we can achieve much more

Percy Hedley Foundation has grown substantially over the years in response to the need for practical support and services for disabled children, adults and their families. We are extremely grateful for all the generous donations we have received that have made these developments possible.

Over the years, thousands of disabled children and adults have learnt to become more independent and are now able to lead fuller and more active lives.

We hope we may count on your continuing support in the future, enabling us to sustain and extend our vital services for disabled people in the region.

For further information please contact

Des Bustard

Tel: 0191 2381321

desbustard@percyhedley.org.uk

Or visit our website:

www.percyhedley.org.uk

Please send donations by post to:

Freepost RSRS-TTYK-YZKG
Fundraising Office
Percy Hedley Foundation
Forest Hall
Newcastle upon Tyne
NE12 8YY

Registered Charity Number 515943

Looking to the Future

Oliver in a IT lesson.

Anthony playing powerchair football.

Alan and Daryn. Alan is a 'Buddy' on the Metro system and supports others to use the service.

This publication has been funded by
The Big Lottery Fund.